L

# Punctuation

*By the same author*

## Little Red Book Series

| | |
|---|---|
| Little Red Book of Slang-Chat Room Slang | Little Red Book of Synonyms |
| Little Red Book of English Vocabulary Today | Little Red Book of Antonyms |
| | Little Red Book of Common Errors |
| Little Red Book of Grammar Made Easy | Little Red Book of Letter Writing |
| Little Red Book of English Proverbs | Little Red Book of Essay Writing |
| Little Red Book of Prepositions | Little Red Book of Word Fact |
| | Little Red Book of Spelling |
| Little Red Book of Idioms and Phrases | Little Red Book of Language Checklist |
| Little Red Book of Effective Speaking Skills | Little Red Book of Perfect Written English |
| Little Red Book of Phrasal Verbs | Little Red Book of Reading and Listening |
| Little Red Book of Euphemisms | Little Red Book of A Child's First Dictionary |
| Little Red Book of Word Power | |
| Little Red Book of Modern Writing Skills | |

## A2Z Book Series

| | |
|---|---|
| A2Z Quiz Book | A2Z Book of Word Origins |

## Others

| | |
|---|---|
| The Book of Fun Facts | The Book of Motivation |
| The Book of More Fun Facts | Read Write Right: Common Errors in English |
| The Book of Firsts and Lasts | |
| The Book of Virtues World Facts Finder | The Students' Companion |

| | |
|---|---|
| Fun Facts: Science | Fun with Maths |
| Fun Facts: Animals | Fun with Numbers |
| Fun Facts: India | Fun with Puzzles |
| Fun Facts: Nature | Fun with Riddles |

# Little Red Book
## *of*
## Punctuation

Terry O'Brien

RUPA

Published by
Rupa Publications India Pvt. Ltd 2012
7/16, Ansari Road, Daryaganj
New Delhi 110002

*Sales centres:*
Allahabad Bengaluru Chennai
Hyderabad Jaipur Kathmandu
Kolkata Mumbai

Copyright © Terry O'Brien 2012

All rights reserved.
No part of this publication may be reproduced, transmitted,
or stored in a retrieval system, in any form or by any means,
electronic, mechanical, photocopying, recording or otherwise,
without the prior permission of the publisher.

ISBN: 978-81-291-2057-1

Third impression 2017

10 9 8 7 6 5 4 3

Terry O'Brien asserts the moral right to be identified
as the author of this work.

Printed at Tara Art Printers Pvt. Ltd., Noida

This book is sold subject to the condition that it shall not, by
way of trade or otherwise, be lent, resold, hired out, or otherwise
circulated, without the publisher's prior consent, in any form of
binding or cover other than that in which it is published.

*I dedicate this book to late Prof. A.P. O'Brien,
my father, friend, guide and mentor, who
inspired me to the canon of excellence:
re-imagining what's essential*

# PREFACE

Punctuation, one is taught, has a point: to keep up law and order. Punctuation marks are the road signs placed along the highway of our communication—to control speeds, provide directions, and prevent head-on collisions. A period has the unblinking finality of a red light; the comma is a flashing yellow light that asks us only to slow down; and the semicolon is a stop sign that tells us to ease gradually to a halt, before gradually starting up again.

The first writing systems were mostly logographic and/or syllabic, for example Chinese and Mayan scripts, and they do not necessarily require punctuation, especially spacing. Even today, formal written modern English differs subtly from spoken English because not all emphasis and disambiguation is possible to convey in print, even with punctuation.

Ancient Chinese classical texts were transmitted without punctuation. The earliest alphabetic writing had no capitalization, no spaces, no vowels and few punctuation marks. This worked as long as the subject matter was restricted to a limited range of topics (e.g., writing used for recording business transactions). Punctuation is historically an aid to reading aloud.

The Greeks were using punctuation marks consisting of vertically arranged dots - usually two (cf. the modern colon) or three - in around the 5th century BC. Greek playwrights such as Euripides and Aristophanes used symbols to distinguish the ends of phrases in written drama: this essentially helped the play's cast to know when to pause. In particular, they used three different symbols to divide speeches, known as commas (indicated by a centred dot), colons(indicated by a dot on the base line), and periods or full stops (indicated by a raised dot).

Punctuation developed dramatically when large numbers of copies of the Christian Bible started to be produced. These were designed to be read aloud and the copyists began to introduce a range of marks to aid the reader, including indentation, various punctuation marks and an early version of initial capitals.

# Punctuation

**PUNCTUATION** (from the Latin *punctum*, a point) is a necessary part of written language. Aristophanes, a grammarian of Alexandria (a. 250 B.C.), introduced some of the first punctuation marks, and the Italian printer Aldus Manutius (A.D. 1450-1515) systematised punctuation and gave it a general usage.

Since then the system has been considerably modified. New developments have taken place, for the fashions of punctuation are always changing. It is thus sometimes difficult to give hard and fast rules. William Cobbett wrote, "Much must be left to taste: something must depend upon the weight which we may wish to give to particular words, or phrases; and something on the seriousness, or the levity, of the subject on which we are writing." Punctuation has already changed since Cobbett's day.

Yet the importance of good punctuation cannot be overemphasized. To regard punctuation as a mere nuisance and necessary evil is quite absurd. As an English Archbishop once declared, "Intellectually, stops matter a great deal. If you are getting your commas, semi-colons and full-stops wrong, it means that you are not getting your thoughts right, and your mind is muddled." The confusing effects of bad punctuation can sometimes be very comic.

Undoubtedly, to punctuate intelligibly is a commercial and social 'basic unit' or 'minimum requirement'; to punctuate well, a social advantage; to punctuate very well, a social and intellectual distinction.

> *NOTE:*
>
> W: ✗
> R: ✓
> C: Comment

## Faulty Stopping

### 1. The Full Stop (.)

(a) Don't fall a victim to what Fowler called "the spot-plague"— the tendency to make full stops do all the work.

✗ Manmohan is here. Manmohan is my cousin. I like him. He likes me. He often comes. We're always pleased to see him. Mother too. Mother fusses over him.

✓ Manmohan, my cousin, is here. We like each other; he often comes and we're always pleased to see him. Mother is pleased too and fusses over him.

C. This kind of writing is often found in inferior journalism. Its effect is staccato and not at all restful, and eventually it defeats its own purpose as it slows down the reader's rate of comprehension instead of' accelerating it.

(b) Don't put a full stop after your signature at the end of a letter or note.

✗ Yours sincerely,
Ravi Dayal.

✓ Your's sincerely,
  Ravi Dayal
(c) Don't insist on putting a full stop after an abbreviation made with the first and last letters of a word, as this is optional.
   e.g.  Mr. Smith or Mr Smith.
         Dr. Shahane or Dr Shahane.

**Comment.** It may be advisable to put a full stop when the abbreviation is a pronounceable word.
   e.g.  Col. (Colonel)
(d) Don't put a full stop at the end of an address, whether on an envelope or at the head of a letter.
✗ 16 Park Street, Calcutta.
✓ 16 Park Street, Calcutta

## 2. The Comma (,)

(a) Don't "comma off" too much and pepper your sentences too liberally with commas.
✗ On his return, he found the letter. Of course, you shall have it. In this way, I can manage it well.
✓ On his return he found the letter. Of course you shall have it. In this way I can manage it well.
C. No comma is necessary after an adverb or adverbial phrase and the words directly following that it qualifies. Only put a comma when it is necessary to avoid confusion or risk of ambiguity.
e.g. (1) Further, punishment is required.
     (2) Further punishment is required.
Here the comma in (1) is necessary to make the meaning clear.
(b) Don't put a comma before "and" or "or" when they join two words, phrases or sentences.

✗   Mirza, and I will go. I like the country in winter, or in summer.

✓   Mirza and I will go. I like the country in winter or in summer.

C.   When there is a series of words or clauses separated by commas with an "and" or "or" linking up the final item, a comma before the last "and" or "or" is optional.

e.g. She visited London, Paris, Rome and Athens.

Or

She visited London, Paris, Rome, and Athens.

I like chocolate, toffee and cake.

Or

I like chocolate, toffee, and, cake.

*Opinions however are divided on this point: some grammarians belong to the "final comma school" and others to the "no-final comma school". A final comma should always be used if it makes the sense clearer.*

e.g. She came with her husband, her sister, and her friend's son.

*NOTE:* Absence of a final comma here would make it ambiguous.

(c)   Don't use a comma to separate a subject from its verb.

✗   We all agreed that jovial, red-faced, bright-eyed Uncle Vivek, was the life and soul of the party.

✓   We all agreed that jovial, red-faced, bright-eyed Uncle Vivek was the life and soul of the party.

C.   If the subject is so long that a comma appears necessary to show that the subject is finished, then the sentence is too clumsy and should be rewritten.

*NOTE:* Don't use a comma to separate verb and object, even when the object is a noun clause.

✗   He shyly asked, if he might have a drink.
✓   He shyly asked if he might have a drink.

(e) Don't put commas between two simple adjectives before a noun.

✗   Her father was a good, kind man.
✓   Her father was a good kind man.

C.  Notice that we say: Her father was good, kind, simple and dutiful.

(f) Never put commas for Defining Relatives and always put commas for Non-defining Relatives.

✗   • My wife who is in Calcutta has written to me. (This suggests that I have a number of wives!)
    • Sailors, who are superstitious, will not sail on a Friday. (This is nonsense too, it suggests all sailors
    • The aeroplane, that will go round the world in two minutes, is not yet constructed. (Also nonsense!)

✓   My wife, who is in Calcutta, has written to me. (Non defining)
    • Sailors who are superstitious will not sail on a Friday. (Defining)
    • The aeroplane that will go round the world in two minutes is not yet constructed. (Defining)

(g) Don't put a comma after the street number of an address. It is quite unnecessary.

✗   36, Akbar Road.
✓   36, Akbar Road

(h) Don't put a comma after the month when date and year are given.

✗   I was born on Sunday, 30 June, 1922. Or I was born on Sunday, June, 30, 1922.
✓   I was born on Sunday, 30 June 1922.
    I was born on Sunday, June 30, 1922.

## 3. The Semi-Colon

Don't be afraid to use the semi-colon, particularly to convey antithesis, or to avoid using too many commas, which may well make a muddle of your sentence.

(a) I admire his intelligence; I detest his character.
(b) The bedroom contained one, wardrobe, one double bed,two chairs, one dressing-table; the nursery, one cot, one chest-of-drawers, two chairs, one rocking-horse; the dining room, six chairs, one table and one sideboard.

*NOTE:* The absence of semi-colons is noticeable in inferior journalism and in the writings of uneducated or half-educated people.

## 4. The Colon

Don't copy the American habit of using a colon at the beginning of a letter.

✗ Dear Sir:With reference to your letter
✓ Dear Sir,With reference to your letter
C. In letters the colon may be used for writing addresses when they are not written on several levels, e.g. 13 Clarence Court: Newbury. Berkshire.

Right use of the colon, like the semi-colon, is a mark of educated writing.

## 5. The Question Mark

(a) Don't use a question mark for indirect questions.
✗ She asked why I was laughing.  She asked why I was laughing.
(b) Don't put a question mark in brackets after a word.
✗ She spoke of the useful (?) work of the committee.

✓   She spoke of the useful work of the committee. (I doubt its usefulness.)

## 6. The Exclamation Mark

Don't overdo this.

✗   "Well! Well! Well!" she said, "I am surprised! I am delighted! I wanted to see you! And here you are!"

✓   "Well, well, well !" she said, "I am surprised and delighted. I wanted to see you and here you are."

C.   Use the exclamation mark only when there is some real emotion to be expressed. When an interjection is repeated several times, separate the words by a comma and place the exclamation mark last.

## 7. The Dash

(a)   Don't use the dash as a maid-of-all-work.

✗   My aunt — a thoughtless creature — never came — never wrote — never even remembered my existence.

✓   My aunt, a thoughtless creature, never came, never wrote, and never even remembered my existence.

*NOTE:* Don't put a comma before a dash.

✗   "To write imaginatively a man should have, — imagination" (J. R. Lowell)

✓   "To write imaginatively a man should have — imagination."

C.   English people treat the dash very badly. Its misuse can be seen in all kinds of writing, from Laurence Sterne's novels to modern newspapers. It is generally employed to save using other punctuation marks, and can frequently be replaced to advantage by brackets or commas. William Cobbett warns us that the dash is "a most perilous thing for a young grammarian to handle".

## 8. The Hyphen

Don't over-hyphen.

✗ The Head-master can come to-day or to-night or at midday to-morrow.

✓ The Headmaster can come today or tonight or at midday tomorrow.

C. There is much confusion here. Remember that pairs of words go through three stages of evolution.

They pass from being (1) Separate words to (2) Hyphenated words and then on to (3) Single words. Words like "midday", "today", "tomorrow" have arrived at stage 3.

Words like "wash-basin", "wrist-watch" are still at stage 2.

Words like " pocket money ", "postal order" are at stage 1.

Some words seem to be kept in all three forms at once e.g. "common sense" or "common-sense" or "commonsense"

Remember that hyphens are usually used with

(a) Compounds of three or more words: forget-me-not, toad-in-the-hole.

(b) Compounds of Verb and Verb, or Verb and Noun: make-believe, kill-joy.

(c) Compounds beginning with the prefixes co-, self-, non-, ex-, vice- and pseudo-: self-love, vice-president, non-smoker.

(d) Adjectival compounds of Noun and Past Participle: heartbroken, home-made.

(e) Compound fractions and compound numerals: two-fifths, sixty-eight, half-term, forty-ninth.

(f)   Compounds that require a hyphen to prevent ambiguity: re-cover (an umbrella) as distinct from     recover (get better), re-creation (of an atmosphere) as distinct from recreation (refreshment).

## 9. Brackets or Parentheses

Don't confuse round brackets and square brackets. Round brackets are the usual form and square ones are used to indicate that there is more of an intrusion than when ordinary brackets are used. They are generally employed in quotations to introduce wordsthat explain the quotation but are no real part of it.

e.g. Kaul says, "He [Kaul's brother] is the greatest liar on earth."

## 10. Inverted Commas or Quotation Marks

(a)   Don't put titles of books, newspapers, periodicals, plays, long poems or ships (of any size!) in inverted commas; they, require italics. Use inverted commas for titles of articles and shot poems, essays, chapters, pictures, songs, names of hotelsand inns. Names ofhouses are often put in quotation marks, but many grammarians, including Fowler, disapprove of this.

(b)   Don't trouble about the distinction between single and double inverted commas. It is merely a matter of convenience to have two kinds when the necessity arises of using one set within another. Formerly double quotation marks were most commonly used, but fashion now favours the use of single quotation marks.

## 11. The Apostrophe

(a)   Don't use an apostrophe for words like "phone" and

"bus", as several names that have been curtailed or beheaded have now established themselves as complete words.

(b) Notice the tendency to drop the apostrophe, especially in plural nouns when the nouns are adjectival and have no real possessive sense, e.g. "Womens Institute", "Boys School", "Students Union" In place-names too, the apostrophe is often omitted.

## 12. Capitals

(a) Don't forget the important distinction between the general and the titular use of proper nouns. Only the latter takes capitals.

✗    There are Professors in every College, and he is professor of English at King's college.

✓    There are professors in every college, and he is Professor of English at King's College.

C.    This also applies to members of the family, e.g. His father and my uncle were at school together.
But
"Hello, Father!" "Goodbye, Uncle Onkar."

(b) Don't forget that most adjectives derived from proper names retain their capital letter, e.g. "A Japanese fan ", "a Miltonic line ".

*Exception.* When the adjective is so generally used that its origin is commonly forgotten, e.g. "Wellington boots".

(c) Don't put small letters for what Webster calls "trademark names". They keep their capitals, e.g. "Ford", "Kodak ", "Hoover".

- ✓ *The Apostrophe(')*
- ✓ *The Comma (,)*
- ✓ *Quotation Marks (") or (" ")*
- ✓ *Capital Letters*
- ✓ *The Full Stop (.)*
- ✓ *The Question Mark (?)*
- ✓ *The Exclamation Mark (!)*
- ✓ *The Colon (:)*
- ✓ *The Semiolon (;)*
- ✓ *Brackets ()*
- ✓ *Square Brackets [ ]*
- ✓ *The Hyphen (-)*
- ✓ *The Dash (—)*
- ✓ *The Slash (/)*

(d)  Don't put small letters for words after "Dear" or "
      dear" at the beginning of a letter. They fake a capital
      capitals, so also does the first word of the letter prope

✗    My Dear auntie,
      how are you?
✓    My dear Auntie,
      How are you?

## 13. italics

(a)  *Don't over-italicize.* Too frequent underlining not only
      defeats its purpose but also offends the eye. As Fowler
      wrote, "To italicize whole sentences or large parts of
      them as a guarantee that some portion of what one has
      written is really worth attending to is a miserable
      confession that the rest is negligible."

(b)  When italicizing titles of books, newspapers or
      periodicals, be careful not to omit the article when it is
      part of the full title.

✗    Carlyle wrote the French Revolution and I saw a
      quotation from it in the Times recently.
✓    Carlyle wrote The French Revolution and I saw a
      quotation from it in The Times recently.

## 14. The Virgule

Don't forget that the virgule, or oblique stroke, is used in
such abbreviations as do (care of), a/c (account) and can
also be employed for writing fractions on the same level
(e.g. 6/7, 4/9) of amounts money, e.g. 4/7s/6d.

# The Apostrophe(')

Misusing or omitting the apostrophe is one of the commonest punctuation errors.

## Showing possession

The apostrophe (') is used to show that something belongs to someone. It is usually added to the end of a word and followed by an *-s*.

**'s is added to the end of singular words:**

- ✓ *a baby's chair*
- ✓ *Harshit's book*
- ✓ *a child's cry*

**'s is added to the end of plural words not ending in -s:**

- ✓ *children's games*
- ✓ *women's clothes*
- ✓ *people's lives*

**An apostrophe alone (') is added to plural words ending in -s:**

- ✓ *Your grandparents are your parents' parents.*
- ✓ *We're campaigning for workers' rights.*
- ✓ *They've hired a new ladies' fashion guru.*

**'s is added to the end of names and singular words ending in -s:**

- ✓ *James's car*
- ✓ *the octopus's tentacles*

However, an apostrophe only is often also used, especially for more formal contexts:

- ✓ *Dickens' novels*
- ✓ *St Giles' Cathedral*

**'s is added to the end of certain professions or occupations to indicate workplaces:**

- ✓ *She's on her way to the doctor's.*
- ✓ *Julie is at the hairdresser's.*

<u>**'s** is added to the end of people or their names to indicate that you are talking about their home:</u>

✓ *I'm going over to Hari's for tea tonight.*

✓ *I popped round to Mum's this afternoon, but she wasn't in.*

<u>**'s** can also be added to:</u>

* whole phrases:

   ✓ *My next-door neighbour's dog was barking away like mad.*

   ✓ *Ratin and Pinky's house was on TV last night.*

* <u>indefinite pronouns such as somebody or anywhere:</u>

   ✓ *Is this anybody's pencil case?*

   ✓ *It's nobody's fault but mine.*

* each other:

   ✓ *We're getting used to each other's habits.*

   ✓ *We kept forgetting each other's names.*

When the possessor is an inanimate object (rather than a living thing), the apostrophe is not used and the word order is changed:

   ✓ *the middle of the street (not the street's middle)*

   ✓ *the front of the house (not the house's front)*

To test whether an apostrophe is in the right place, think about who the owner is:

   ✓ the boy's books (= the books belonging to the boy)

   ✓ the boys' books (= the books belonging to the boys)

### Key points to remember

   ✓ An apostrophe is *not* used to form possessive pronouns such as *its, yours,* or *theirs.*

   ✓ An apostrophe is *not* used to form the plurals of words such as *potatoes* or *tomatoes.*

### With letters and numbers

An apostrophe is used in front of two figures referring to a year or decade:

✓ Assam students rioted in **'98** (short for '1998').
✓ He worked as a schoolteacher during the **'60s** and early **'90s.**

An apostrophe can be used in plurals of letters and numbers to make them more readable:

✓ Mind your p**'s** and q**'s.**
✓ His 2**'s** look a bit like 7**'s.**
✓ She got straight A**'s** in her exams.

**Key point to remember**
✓ it's = it is, e.g. *It's a holiday today.*
✓ its = belonging to it, e.g. *The dog was scratching its ear.*

## Contracted forms

An apostrophe is used in shortened forms of words to show that one or more letters have been missed out. Contractions are usually shortened forms of auxiliary verbs:

| **be** | **have** |
|---|---|
| I**'m** | I/we/they**'ve** (have) |
| we/you/they**'re** (are) | he/she/it/one**'s** (has) |
| He/she/it/one**'s** (is) | I/we/you/he/she/it/one/they**'d** (had) |

**would**
I/we/you/he/she/it/one/they**'d** (would)
or the negative not:

**not**
we/you/they are**n't**
He/she/it/one is**n't**
I/we/they have**n't**
He/she/it/one has**n't**

In order to work out what the contracted forms **'s** and **'d** represent, you need to look at what follows it:

If **'s** is followed by an *-ing* form, it represents the auxiliary *is*.
- ✓ *She's **reading** a book about the ancient Egyptians.*
- ✓ *He's **going** to Oman for his holidays.*

If **'s** is followed by an adjective or a noun phrase, it represents the main verb **is**:
- ✓ *She's **nervous** about meeting my parents.*
- ✓ *He's **brilliant** at language.*

If **'s** is followed by a past participle, it can represent is as it is used in the passive:
- ✓ *He's **portrayed** by the media as a kindly old man.*
- ✓ *It's often **said** that film stars are frustrated actors.*

or *has* it is used in the present perfect:
- ✓ *She's **broken** her wrist.*
- ✓ *It's **been** ages since we last saw you.*

If **'s** is followed by *got*, it represents the auxiliary *has*:
- ✓ *She's **got** two brothers and one sister.*
- ✓ *It's **got** everything you could want.*

If **'d** is followed by a past participle, it represents the auxiliary *had*:
- ✓ *I'd **raced** against him before, but never in a marathon.*
- ✓ *She couldn't believe what she'd **done**.*

If **'d** is followed by a base form, it represents the modal auxiliary would:
- ✓ *I'd **give up** now, if I were you.*
- ✓ *When we were kids we'd **spend** hours out on our bikes.*

If **'d** is followed by *rather* or *better*, it represents the modal auxiliary would:
- ✓ *We'd **better** go home soon.*
- ✓ *I'd **rather** not talk about that.*

# The Comma (,)

The comma marks a short pause between parts of a sentence.

## Separating main clauses

Main clauses (main parts of sentences) that are joined together with *and* or *but* do not normally have a comma before the conjunction unless the two clauses have different subjects:

- ✓ *You go out of the door and turn immediately left.*
- ✓ *It was cold outside, but we decided to go out for a walk anyway.*

## Separating subordinate clauses from main clauses

Commas are normally used if the subordinate clause (the part of the sentence that is not the main part) comes before the main clause:

- ✓ *If you have any problems, just call me.*
- ✓ *Just call me if you have any problems.*

Sometimes a comma is used even when the main clause comes first, if the clauses are particularly long:

- ✓ *We should be able to finish the work by the end of the week.*
- ✓ *If nothing unexpected turns up between now and then.*

## Separating relative clauses from main clauses

Commas are used to mark off non-defining relative clauses. This is the type of clause that adds to information about a noun or noun phrase:

- ✓ *My next-door neighbour, who works from home, is keeping an eye on the house while we're away.*
- ✓ *She moved to Mumbai, where she was immediately signed as a singer songwriter.*

Commas are not required in defining relative clauses (clauses that say Who or what something is):

- ✓ *Let's make sure the money goes to the people **who need it most**.*
- ✓ *The computer **(that) I borrowed** kept on crashing.*

**Separating items in a list**

Commas are used to separate three or more items in a list or series:

  ✓ *She got out bread, butter, and jam (but bread and butter).*

Note that the comma is often not given before the final *and* or *or*:

  ✓ *They breed dogs, cats, rabbits and hamsters.*

  ✓ *We did canoeing, climbing and archery.*

**Separating adjectives**

Commas are often used between adjectives, whether they come before the noun or after a linking verb:

  ✓ *It was a hot, dry and dusty road.*

  ✓ *It's wet, cold and windy outside.*

A comma is not usually used before an adjective that is followed by *and*.

**With adverbials**

When an adverbial such as however, therefore or unfortunately refers to a whole sentence, it is separated from the rest of the sentence by a comma:

  ✓ *However, police would not confirm this rumour.*

  ✓ *Therefore, I try to avoid using the car as much as possible.*

**With question tags and short answers**

Commas are used before question tags and after yes or no in short answers:

  ✓ *It's quite cold today, isn't it?*

  ✓ *He's up to date with all his injections, isn't he?*

  ✓ *Are you the mother of these children? — Yes, I am.*

  ✓ *You're Minoo Chopra, aren't you?— No, I'm not.*

## With names

Commas are used to separate the name of a person or group being spoken to from the rest of the sentence:

✓ *And now, ladies and gentlemen, please raise your glasses in a toast to the happy couple.*

✓ *Come on, Lata, be reasonable.*

✓ *Dad, can you come and help me, please?*

## With discourse markers

Commas are used to separate discourse markers (spoken phrases, often with little meaning, that people use before or between parts of sentences) from the rest of the sentence:

✓ *Well, believe it or not; I actually passed!*

✓ *Now then, let's see what's on TV tonight.*

✓ *Actually, I quite enjoyed it.*

## In reported speech

Commas are used to follow direct speech (if there is no question or exclamation mark after the quotation), or to show that it comes next:

✓ *'I don't understand this question,' said Peter.*

✓ *Peter said, 'I don't understand this question.'*

✓ *'You're crazy!' Claire exclaimed.*

✓ *What do you think you're doing?' Dad bellowed.*

It is also possible to punctuate reported speech of the type *Ravi said,'…'* using a colon instead of a comma. This is a particularly common practice in American English:

✓ *Ravi said: 'Dream on.'*

## In dates

A comma must be used between the day of the month and the year, when the two numbers are next to each other:

✓ *March 31, 2011*

# Quotation Marks ('') or ("")

## Direct Speech

Direct speech gives the actual words that a speaker used. It is common in novels and other writing where the words of a speaker are quoted.

The words spoken are enclosed in single or double quotation marks:

- ✓ **'Have you been to the new shopping precinct yet?'** enquired Shona.
- ✓ **'I've already seen it,'** John replied.

The comma comes inside the quotation marks, unless the reporting verb is positioned inside a reported sentence that itself does not require a comma:

- ✓ *'There is', Anita said, 'nothing we can do about it.'*

## Other uses

Single quotation marks are sometimes used:

- to draw attention to a word
  - ✓ The word **'book'** can be used as a noun or a verb.

Verbs such as **'criticize'** can be spelled with an 's' or a 'z'.

- to indicate an unusual use of a word
  - ✓ She pointed out that websites used for internet voting could be **'spoofed'**.
  - ✓ You could go to one of those parties where you swap (or **'swish'**) clothes.
- to suggest that the writer wants to be distanced from a word.
  - ✓ I think he's too mean to go away on holiday, but he insists on calling it a **'stay stations.'**
  - ✓ I keep reading about **'dress fatigue'** in fashion magazines.

Note that the full stop comes after the quotation marks in such cases.

# Capital Letters

A capital (or 'upper case') letter is used to mark the beginning of a sentence.

✓ *When he was 20, I dropped out of university and became a model.*

Capital letters are also used for the first letter in proper nouns.

These include:

- people's names:
  Jessica Lal                    William Davidson
- days of the week
  Wednesday                      Saturday
- months of the year
  August                         January
- public holidays
  Christmas                      Diwali
- nationalities
  Indian                         Iraqi
- languages
  Urdu                           Flemish
- geographical locations
  Australia                      New Zealand
  Mount Everest                  The Mediterranean Sea
- company names
  Rupa & Co                      Microsoft & CO
- religions
  Islam                          Buddhism

Capital letters are also used for the first letter in titles of books, magazines, newspapers, TV shows, films, etc. Where there are several words, a capital letter is usually used for all the main content words in the title (i.e. not the prepositions or the determiners — unless they are the first word in the title)

Capital letters are also used for the first letter in titles of books, magazines, newspapers, TV shows, films, etc. Where there are several words, a capital letter is usually used for all the main content words in the title (i.e. not the prepositions or the determiners — unless they are the first word in the title).

| | |
|---|---|
| ✓ The Times | Hello! |
| ✓ Twelfth Night | The Secret Garden |
| ✓ Newsnight | Mamma Mia! |

# The Full Stop (.)

Full stops are used:
- to mark the end of a sentence
  - ✓ *Let's have some lunch.*
  - ✓ *I have to catch a bus in ten minutes.*
- to mark the end of a sentence fragment
  - ✓ *Are you cold?-Yes, a bit.*
  - ✓ *Do you like this sort of music? Not really.*
- in initials for people's names, although this practice is becoming less frequent
  - ✓ *T. J. O'Brien*          *Colin M. Barnes*
  - ✓ *M.C. Hammer*            *Ronald G. Hardie*
- after abbreviations, although this practice is becoming less frequent
  - ✓ *P.S. do pop in next time you're passing.*
  - ✓ *She's moved to the I.T. department.*
  - ✓ *R.S.V.P. to Harish Mehta on 011-2442321*
  - ✓ *The U.S. government reacted strongly to the accusation.*

When an abbreviation consists of a shortened word such as *Rev.* or *Prof.* a full stop is needed.

*Prof. John Dayal will be speaking on the subject of literature.*

*Flight BA 345: dep. 09.44 arr. 11.10.*

When an abbreviation contains the last letter of the shortened word, a full stop is not needed.
- ✓ **Dr** *McDonald 41,*   **St** *Mary's School*
- ✓ *Daryagang* **Rd**      *Navketan Pictures (India)***Ltd**

Note that full stops are not used in many common sets of initials:
- ✓ Did you see that programme on **NDTV** last night?
- ✓ Millions of people now call the **NHS** Direct helpline each year.

or at the end of headlines, headings and titles:

- ✓ *Fear grips global stock markets*
- ✓ *Teaching grammar as a liberating force*
- ✓ *Pride and Prejudice*

Remember that a full stop, and not a question mark, is used after an indirect question or a polite request:

- ✓ *He asked if the bus had left.*
- ✓ *Will you open your books on page 14.*
- ✓ *I wonder what's happened.*
- ✓ *She asked him where he was going.*

In American English, the full stop is called a **period**.

# The Question Mark (?)

The question mark marks the end of a question:

  ✓ *When will we be arriving?*
  ✓ *Why did you do that?*
  ✓ *Does any of this matter?*
  ✓ *He's certain to be elected, isn't he?*

Question marks are used in direct questions, i.e. when the actual words of a speaker are used. A reported question should end with a full stop:

  ✓ *The lady said, 'Where are you going ?*
  ✓ *The lady asked where she was going.*

Note that you put a question mark at the end of a question, even if the words in the sentence are not in the normal question order, or some words are omitted. Care is needed here as such a sentence can look, at first sight, like a statement rather than a question:

  ✓ *You know he doesn't live here any longer?*

A full stop, rather than a question mark, is used after an indirect question:

  ✓ *I'd like to know what you've been doing all this time.*
  ✓ *I wonder what's happened.*

A full stop also replaces a question mark at the end of a sentence which looks like a question if, in fact, it is really a polite request:

  ✓ *Will you please return the completed forms to me.*
  ✓ *Would you please call my brother and ask him to collect my car.*

# The Exclamation Mark (!)

The exclamation mark is used after exclamations and emphatic expressions:

- ✓ *I can't believe it!*
- ✓ *Oh, no! Look at this mess!*

> *NOTE:*
> The exclamation mark loses its effect if it is overused.
> It is better to use a full stop after a sentence expressing
> mild excitement or humour.

- ✓ *It was such a beautiful day.*
- ✓ *I felt like such a fool.*

# The Colon (:)

The colon indicates a break between two main clauses which is stronger than a comma but weaker than a full stop.

A colon is used:

* in front of a list
  * ✓ *I used three colours: green, blue and pink.*
  * ✓ *Make sure you wear clothes made from natural fibres: cotton, silk and wool.*

* in front of an explanation or a reason
  * ✓ *Nevertheless, the main problem remained: what should be done with the two men?*
  * ✓ *I decided against going away this weekend: the weather forecast was dreadful.*

* after introductory headings
  * ✓ *Cooking time: about five minutes.*
  * ✓ *Start time: 10 o'clock.*

* in more formal writing, between two main clauses that are connected
  * ✓ *It made me feel claustrophobic: what, I wonder, would happen to someone who was really unable to tolerate being locked into such a tiny space?*
  * ✓ *Be patient: the next book in the series has not yet been published.*

* in front of the second part of a book title
  * ✓ *Farming and wildlife: a study in compromise*
  * ✓ *Beyond single words: the most frequent collocations in spoken English*

* to introduce direct speech, especially in American English, or when the quotation is particularly long

✓ *He said: 'You owe me three thousand and twenty-five rupees.'*
✓ *The Health Minister said: 'The health I.T. programme will mean that patients will get access to more comprehensive information to help them make choices.'*

# The Semiolon (;)

The semicolon is used to mark a break between two main clauses when there is a balance or a contrast between the clauses,

Compare:

✓ *The engine roared into life. The propellers began to turn*

✓ *The plane taxied down the runway ready for takeoff*

with:

o *The engine roared into life; the propellers began to turn; the plane taxied down the runway ready for takeoff*

A useful test to work out when to use a semicolon is to ask yourself whether the two clauses could be written instead as separate sentences. If the answer is 'yes', then you can use a semicolon.

*Note* that it is quite acceptable to use a full stop in these cases, but a semicolon is preferable if you wish to convey the sense of a link or continuity between the parts of your sentence:

✓ *I'm not that interested in jazz; I prefer classical music.*

✓ *He knew everything about me; I had never even heard of him.*

A semicolon is also used to separate items in a list, especially if the listed items are phrases or clauses, which may already contain commas:

✓ *The holiday was a disaster: the flight was four hours late; the hotel, which was described as 'luxury' was dirty; and it rained for the whole fortnight.*

# Brackets ()

Brackets (also called parentheses) are used to enclose a word or words which can be left out and still leave a meaningful sentence:

✓ *The wooded area (see map below) is approximately 4,000 hectares. This is a process which Hayek (a writer who came to rather different conclusions) also observed.*

Brackets are also used to show alternatives or options:

✓ *Any student(s) interested in taking part should email me.*

✓ *A goat should give from three to six pints (1.7 to 3.4 litres) of milk a day.*

Note that when the structure of the sentence as a whole demands punctuation after a bracketed section, the punctuation is given outside the brackets:

✓ *I haven't yet spoken to John (I mean John Maple, my boss), but I have a meeting with him on Friday.*

✓ *For lunch we had sandwiches (pastrami on rye and so on), salami, coleslaw, fried chicken, and potato salad.*

Punctuation is given before the closing brackets only when it applies to the bracketed section rather than to the sentence as a whole:

✓ *He's very handsome (positively gorgeous in fact!) and still single.*

# Square
# Brackets [ ]

Square brackets are used, usually in books and articles, when supplying words that make a quotation clearer or that comment on it, although they were not originally said or written:

 ✓ *Mr. Russie Modi concluded: 'The novel is at its strongest when describing the dignity of Cambridge [ a slave ] and the education of Emily (the daughter of an absentee landlord).'*

Square brackets with dots are used to show where some words have been missed out:

 ✓ *Greg Smith, chief executive of Pharm-wise[... ], addressed the meeting.*

# The Hyphen (-)

The hyphen joins words or parts of words.

Hyphens are used at the ends of lines where a word has been split, to warn the reader that the word continues on the next line. If the word you need to split is clearly made up of two or more smaller words or elements, you should put the hyphen after the first of these parts.

Otherwise, you put the hyphen at the end of a syllable:

| | |
|---|---|
| *wheel-barrow* | *inter-national* |
| *listen-ing* | *compli-mentary* |
| | *infor-mation* |

It is best not to add a hyphen if the word is a short one, or if it would mean writing just one or two letters at the end or beginning of a line. For example, it would be better to write 'unnatural' on the line below, rather than writing 'un-' on one line and 'natural' on the next line below, rather than writing 'un-' on one line and 'natural' on the next.

Prefixes that are used in front of a word beginning with a capital letter always have a hyphen after them:

> *a wave of anti-British feeling*
> *a neo-Byzantine cathedral*

A hyphen is used to join two or more words that together form an adjective, where this adjective is used before the noun it describes:

✓ *an up-to-date account*
✓ *a last-minute rush*
✓ *a six-year-old boy*

The hyphen is omitted when the adjective so formed comes after the noun or pronoun it describes:

> *The accounts are up to date.*
> *It was all rather last minute.*
> *He's six years old.*

Some common compound nouns are usually written with hyphens:

> *mother-in-law*        *great-grandmother*

Hyphens can be used to split words that have been formed by adding a prefix to another word, especially to avoid an awkward combination of letters or confusion with another word:

> *re-elect*
> *re-covering furniture*
> *re-creation*

# The Dash (—)

A spaced dash (i.e. with a single space before and after it) is used:

- at the beginning and end of a comment that interrupts the flow of a sentence
  - ✓ *Now children — Kripal, stop that immediately! — open your books on page 20.*
- to separate off extra information
  - ✓ *Boots and shoes — all shapes, sizes and colours — tumbled out.*

An unspaced dash (i.e. with no space before or after it) is used:

- to indicate a range
  *pages 54-72*
- between two adjectives or noun modifiers (nouns that go before other nouns) that indicate that two countries or groups are involved in something or that an individual has two roles or aspects
- *Swedish—Norwegian relations improved, the United States—Canada free trade pact a mathematician—philosopher*
- to indicate that something such as a plane or a train goes between two places
- the Kolkota—Mumbai flight
- the New Delhi—Lahore train

# The Slash (/)

The slash separates letters, words or numbers. It is used to indicate alternatives, ratios and ranges, and in website addresses:

- *he/she/it*
- *200 km/hr*
- *the 2001/02 accounting year*
- *http://www.abcdefg.com*

# Punctuation Is a Skill
### Stops, Commas and Other Marks

*Sentences start with a Capital letter,*
*So as to make your writing better.*
*Use a full stop to mark the end —*
*It closes every sentence penned.*

## Rules of Punctuation

Punctuation is the clear presentation of the written language. Punctuation is a courtesy designed to help readers to understand a story without stumbling.

It may help you to know something about its past. Two centuries ago most punctuation took its cues from speech. This was a period when the predominant practice of reading aloud, with its pauses and dramatic stresses, was translated into written punctuation — rhetorical punctuation.

A hundred years on, with increased literacy the spoken word gave way to the written. The stress now was on meaning rather than dramatic effect, and rhetorical (or oratorical) punctuation bowed to a more logical system.

Today we have a blend of both: a system capable of conveying force, intonation, urgency, tension, rhythm and passion while never abandoning its duty to consistency and clarity of meaning.

Punctuation probably reached its zenith in the late 19th century helping to make sense of fashionably-long sentences. The rules were fairly rigid, too. Now, the grammatical rules are more relaxed. Sentences, heavily influenced by the brevity of much newspaper usage, are shorter; the need for the complicated division of long sentences has disappeared. Commas are freely dropped where the meaning remains unaffected. The full stops after an abbreviation are disappearing in a general quest for typographic neatness.

Most people using the English language probably go through life without ever putting on paper any punctuation marks other than the comma, dash and full stop.

If your knowledge of this art is full of holes, or a bit rusty, here's a brief refresher course that should help banish confusion with capitals, hassles with hyphens and catastrophes with apostrophes.

## Units of Space: sentences and paragraphs

Space is a basic form of punctuation. It separates words, sentences, paragraphs and larger units of writing such as chapters.

The sentence is about the most common of all grammatical units.

What is a sentence? A sentence should express a single idea, complete in thought and construction. Like this:

The rare great crested newt was once called the great warty newt.

The sentence can be quite elastic, and punctuation allows us to expand it:

The rare great crested newt, which is native to Britain and rarely exceeds fifteen centimetres in length, was once called the great warty newt.

You'll notice how the commas have allowed us to double the length of the sentence, adding fresh information without losing any of its original clarity. But sentences can also shrink, sometimes alarmingly:

Don't!

That single word, provided it is given meaning by other words or thoughts surrounding it, is a sentence, or, more correctly, a sentence fragment:

I went over to the door and tried to open it.

Don't!

I spun around, searching for the owner of the angry voice. In the darkness, a face appeared...

You can see here that not only the surrounding words, but also a range of spaces and punctuation marks, help to give that single word the meaning intended.

A question that crops up with regularity is, 'How long should a sentence be?' The answer is, neither too long nor too short. Short sentences are easier to take but an endless succession of staccato sentences can irritate the reader. Conscientious writers will read their work aloud or mentally aloud as they proceed; that way the sentences are likely to form themselves into a logical, interesting, economical and, with luck, elegant flow of thought.

Here are some useful pointers.

## Capital Letters

Capital letters are a form of punctuation in that they help to guide the eye and mind through a text.

## Devices for Separating and Joining
## The Full Stop

We now shrink from the paragraph to a minuscule dot: the full stop, full point or period. Minuscule it may be, but it packs a potent power. The full stop is the most emphatic, abrupt and unambiguous of all the punctuation marks.

Full stops control the length of your sentences, so remember:

- Try to keep sentences variable in length, but generally short.
- Using long sentences doesn't necessarily make you a better writer.
- To use only full stops is as unnatural as walking without bending your legs.

## The Comma

The comma is the most flexible and most versatile of all the punctuation marks. And because it is the least emphatic mark it is also the most complex and subtle. Not surprisingly, many writers feel a nagging uncertainty about using commas.

Using commas effectively to make your writing more readable is a bit of a balancing act that requires thought and practice.

*Some writers over-use commas*

✓ It is, curiously, surprising when, say, you hear your name announced in a foreign language, or even in a strange accent.

Although grammatically correct that sentence seems to be hedged with ifs, buts, maybes and pontifications. Can it be rewritten without losing the meaning?

The sentence, less two commas, is now a little more direct. Here's another sample, which can be rewritten without using any commas at all:

✓ He had not, previously, met the plaintiff except when, in 1994, he had, unexpectedly, found himself in Jaipur.

## The Functions of the Comma

- **Setting apart names and persons:**
  Are you going to meet him tomorrow, Rohit?
  That, ladies and gentlemen, is the situation.
  Darling, don't you think you've gone too far?

- **Itemising words:**
  Please place all towels, costumes, clothing and valuables in the lockers.

- **Itemising word groups:**
  Please place any articles of clothing, swimming and sporting equipment, personal belongings, but not money and jewellery, in the lockers.

- **Enclosing additional thoughts or qualifications:**
  The occasion was, on the whole, conducted with great dignity. The class thought it was, arguably, one of his finest novels.

- **Setting apart interjections:**
  Look, I've had enough!
  Oh. Have it your way, then!

**Indicating pauses before direct speech:**
Kripal turned abruptly and said, 'If that's the way you feel, then go home!'

- **Introducing questions:**
  You will be going soon, won't you?
  She is marrying Kirpal next month, isn't she?
- **Emphasising points of view:**
  Naturally, I'll look after her.
  Of course, she fully deserves the prize.
- **Setting off comparative or contrasting statements:**
  The taller they are, the farther they fall.
  The more he adored her, the less she cared.
- **Reinforcing statements:**
  She's ill because she simply won't eat, that's why!
  It'll come right in the end, I'm sure.

## Using Commas with Adjectives

*NOTE:* one has the adjectives separated by commas, and the other does not:

✓ The night resounded with a loud, chilling, persistent ringing. It was a large brick Victorian mansion.

The reasons are embodied in two seemingly simple rules worth remembering:

- Where the adjectives (or other modifiers) define separate attributes (loud, chilling, persistent), they are best separated by commas.

- Where the adjectives work together to create a single image (large, brick, Victorian), the commas are best avoided.

Two seemingly simple rules, but they can be tricky to apply. Sometimes you may be led into ambiguity, and have to resort to common sense:

Myra was a pretty smart, young woman.

Myra was a pretty smart young woman.

Well, does the writer mean that Myra was pretty and smart, or just very smart?

## The Oxford, or Final Comma

*The Times* advises its journalists to avoid the so-called Oxford comma:

x, y and z and not x, y, and z. What this means is that:

Martin spoke to Edith, Lesley, Bunty and Samantha.

## is preferred to

Martin spoke to Edith, Lesley, Bunty, and Samantha.

A final comma before and in a list is now outmoded unless there is the possibility of ambiguity:

The colours are red, blue and white.

Does this mean three separate colours, or two — red, and blue and white in some sort of combination? It's possible, so in this case a comma after blue might be wise to make sure that everyone gets the message that we're talking about three colours.

## Other Problem Comma Placements

It has been customary to enclose adverbs and adverbial
phrases (however, indeed, for example, anyway, on the
contrary etc.) with commas:

✓ You are, nevertheless, guilty of the first charge.

However the trend today is to dispense with such commas
if the meaning of a statement is clear without them:

• You are nevertheless guilty of the first charge.

But always read over such sentences carefully to avoid
ambiguous dangers such as:

The hospital informed us that both victims were happily
recovering

• What was really meant was:

The hospital informed us that both victims were, happily,
recovering,

You'll also find that commas are needed for sentences
beginning with adverbs, such as:

• Curiously, the two scientists had never met.

Sometimes you will find that verbs will need enclosing
by commas to help guide readers through a complex passage:

• In the daytime, sleeping, the baby was adorable, but at
  nights, howling continuously, she was a tyrant and a
  monster.

One of the most common instances of misplacement
occurs when a comma is inserted before an and when,
logically, it should have been dropped in after:

✘ He glanced at the clock, and abruptly closing his book,
  leapt up from the chair.

✓ He glanced at the clock and, abruptly closing his book,
  leapt up from the chair.

## Using Commas as Parenthesis

One of the most interesting, but also perhaps the most contentious, use of commas, is to parenthesise (or bracket) relevant but not essential matter from the main part of a sentence:

The wild hyacinths (which are now at the height of their season) tint the woods with a pale blue mist.

The essential message here is *The wild hyacinths tint the woods with a pale blue mist*. But then we've had a further thought — which are now at the height of their season — which we'd like to include in the same sentence. Sometimes we enclose such additions in parenthesis (brackets) as above, but mostly we use a pair of far more convenient and less disruptive commas:

✓ The wild hyacinths, which are now at the height of their season, tint the woods with a pale blue mist.

*Where a phrase or clause does not define or qualify the subject, indicate that it is non-essential matter by isolating it with a pair of commas. Where a phrase or clause defines or qualifies the subject, weld it to the subject by omitting the commas.*

## The Semicolon

Semicolons make some writers nervous but once you get the hang of them you'll find they are very useful punctuation marks. They have a number of grammar and style functions:

• **Using semicolons to join words, word groups and sentences**

Occasionally we find ourselves writing a long sentence with

too many connecting words such as and, but and also, with the danger of getting into an impossible tangle:

The history of the semicolon and colon is one of confusion because there are no precise rules governing their use and, furthermore, many writers would argue that both marks are really stylistic rather than parenthetical, and that they can easily be replaced by commas, full stops and dashes, and there the argument rests.

There's nothing grammatically wrong with that but it is unwieldy and unappealing to both eye and mind. Many writers would, without much hesitation, recast it as two or more separate sentences:

The history of the semicolon and colon is one of confusion; there are no precise rules governing their use; many writers argue that both marks are really stylistic rather than parenthetical and that they can easily be replaced by commas, full stops or dashes; and there the argument rests.

### Using semicolons to separate word groups containing commas

Any sentence that is essentially a list should be crystal clear and easily read. Most 'sentence lists' adequately separate the items with commas, but sometimes the items themselves are groups containing commas and require semicolons for clarity. These two examples demonstrate how handy semicolons can be:

Those present included Mr and Mrs Minu, their daughters Shikha, Charu and Savita; the Smith twins; Reg and Paul Watson; Joyce Helen and Bill Hobson; etc.

*Semicolons can restore order to a sentence suffering from 'Comma Riot'*

*Using semicolons to provide pauses before certain adverbs*

There are certain adverbs and conjunctions that require a preceding pause, but one longer and stronger than that provided by a comma.

*Look at this example:*

**With a Comma:** It was a beautiful car, moreover it was economical to run.

**With a Semicolon:** It was a beautiful car; moreover it was economical to run.

You can see and hear that need for a pause before moreover, can't you? A comma is wrong for both grammar and rhetoric. Here's another example; read it and note your instinctive pause before nevertheless:

Milkha Singh claimed he'd beaten the bookies on every race; nevertheless he was broke as usual when he left the track.

Watch out for *therefore, however, besides, also, moreover, furthermore, hence, consequently and subsequently*; in many constructions they will require a preceding semicolon.

## Trouble with your Colon?

Although under threat from the dash, the colon is a versatile workhorse, and many colon-doubters are stopped in their tracks when confronted with the range of its functions.

- **Using the colon to point the reader's attention forward**
  In this role the colon acts as a pointing finger, as if to warn the reader about a statement ahead: 'Wait for it . . here it comes!'

- **Using the colon to introduce a list**
  This is perhaps where colons are most commonly used:
  The hotel had everything: pool, sauna, Jacuzzi, gym,
  hairdresser, tanning booths and even a dietician.
- **Using the colon to present an explanation or example**
  The beleaguered bank closed its doors after just three
  days: not surprising when you saw the list of directors.
- **Using the colon to introduce direct speech**
  Although most stylists insist that commas are the correct
  marks to introduce direct speech, the use of colons today
  hardly earns a frown:
  The Minister strode up to the platform, opened his notes
  and glared at the assembly: 'You have not come here
  tonight for nothing,' he growled.
- **Using the colon to present a conclusion**
  Fifty-three years in the business suggested to him there
  was only one certainty in life: the inevitability of change.
- **Using the colon as a substitute for a conjunction**
  Rajiv downed him with a dazzling left hook that came
  from nowhere: if any man did not get up.
- **Using colons to introduce questions, quotations and
  subtitles**
  The essential question is simply this: did she or did she
  not cheat Mr Thakur?
- **Using the colon to link contrasting statements**
  In this role the colon steps into the ring with the semi-
  colon, which also has the ability to administer a mild
  shock. The choice is a matter of taste:
  She cooks: I eat.
  Jeremy had only one small fault: he was an inveterate
  liar.

*NOTE:*
- The difference between a colon and a semicolon is not a difference in 'weight or force; the two marks are mostly used for quite different purposes
- A colon is never followed by a capital letter, except with proper nouns: Minu Chopra, Tata Motor Co, etc.

And also take note that the colon is widely misused, or used unnecessarily as in this example:

✘ The man was amazing and was able to play: the piano, violin, double bass, trombone, clarinet, harp and drums.

## The Embrace of the Bracket

What's the difference between commas and brackets? Generally, material within commas is still very much part of the sentence, and must observe the grammatical conventions of the sentence. Bracketed material, on the other hand, is more distanced from the main sentence. Brackets also release the writer from a lot of responsibility. The parenthesised material, leading a 'separate life', is not required grammatically to match the sentence into which it is inserted.

The bracket's embrace is extremely adaptable, as the following catalogue of examples of usage demonstrates:

- **ADDING INFORMATION**
- **EXPLANATION**
- **AFTERTHOUGHT**
- **CLARIFICATION**
- **COMMENT**
- **ILLUSTRATION**

## The Square Bracket

Square brackets are not angular versions of parentheses; they have a different function entirely. Unlike matter within round brackets, words enclosed in square brackets are intended to be not part of a sentence, but an editorial or authorial insert:

It was a matter of opinion that if offered the position, he [Professor Bhattacharya] would most likely refuse it on moral grounds.

That sentence came at the end of a very long paragraph.

*NOTE:* The professor's name had been mentioned at the beginning, but other names and a lot of discussion followed so that the late reference to he was in danger of being misunderstood. The editor therefore inserted the name [Professor Bhattacharya] in square brackets to remove any doubt and also to indicate that the intervention was the editor's and not the author's.

One of the most common uses of square brackets is to enclose the adverb sic (from the Latin sicut, meaning 'just as') to indicate that incorrect or doubtful matter is quoted exactly from the original:

Miss Pinky Goel [sic] with her fiance Mr Goving Ram.

## A Dash

Although the dash is a mark much disliked — it has in recent times attracted a growing band of defenders.

Others admire the dash for its flexibility and disdain for rules.

Here are some of the respectable ways in which the dash
will be found useful:

- LINKING DEVICE

Mrs Sharma had four young
daughters — Poonam
Manju, Preety and Payal.

- AS A PAUSE

Everyone expected the
speaker to be controversial
— but not to the extent of
swearing.

- SIGNALLING SURPRISE

A straight line is the shortest
distance between

- OR PARADOX

two points — when you're
sober.

- INDICATING

There will be, of course, er
— a small charge, because
—

- HESITATION

well, er –

- SEPARATING LISTS

She assembled all the
ingredients — flour, sugar,
eggs, and raisins — and
started on the pudding.

- AFTERTHOUGHTS

They babbled on, delighted
at sighting the rare parakeet
— I didn't see so much as a
feather.

*NOTE:* If you use dashes to set apart (as in separating
lists), remember to insert the second dash, and not a
comma or semicolon.

## Quotation Marks

Quotation marks or 'inverted commas'. If you look at a newspaper or book and examine these marks closely you'll see that only the opening mark is inverted — that is, with the 'tail of the tadpole' pointing up; the closing mark is a normal raised or hanging comma or pair of commas. So we should use the term quotation marks (or quotes for short) exclusively.

Another point about quotation marks is whether to use single ('single') marks or double ("double") marks:

- Harish said flatly 'I never want to see him again.'
- Harish said flatly "I never want to see him again."

*NOTE:* Newspapers and book publishers are divided on this; some use single quotes, others double. It's a matter of taste. But whether you use single or double marks you need to be aware of the convention for enclosing a quote within a quote. If you pefer single quotes, a quote within a quote must use double quotes. And vice versa:

The sales assistant said, 'We only have them in grey and blue but yesterday my boss told me, "I don't know why they don't make them in other colours."'

On the very rare occasions where it is found necessary to have a third quote within a second quote in the same sentence, the formula is single! double/single, or double/single/double.

## Quoting Direct Speech

When we read a newspaper report or story we want to know when we're reading reported or interpreted speech and when we're reading words actually spoken.

**Quotation marks help us to differentiate between the two forms:**

Mr Majid said that in his view the value of the rupee would drop towards the end of the year. 'I also believe most European currencies will follow suit,' he added.

> *NOTE:* This tells us that the writer has summarised the first part of the statement in his own words, and we have to accept that his summary is a correct version of what Mr Majid said.

It is also vital to make sure your reader knows who is responsible for the quoted statement. This is usually accomplished with what is called a reporting clause, which can introduce the statement or follow it or even interrupt it:

1. Jatin stated, 'I am innocent and I can easily prove it.'
2. 'I am innocent and I can easily prove it,' Jatin stated.
3. 'I am innocent,' Jatin stated, 'and I can easily prove it.'

Another point to remember is that when quoted speech is interrupted by a reporting clause, two rules apply.

If the quoted statement is interrupted at the end of a sentence it should be finished with a comma and resumed with a capital letter:

'I knew I'd seen that bird before,' said Gita. 'It was a mynah, wasn't it?'

But if the speech is interrupted mid-sentence, it should be resumed in lower-case:

'Don't you agree,' asked Gita, 'that the bird over there is a mynah?'

## How to Close Quotations

It is easy to remind writers not to forget to close their quotations. What is a little more difficult is . . . how? Look at this example:

He then asked her, 'Do you think I'm drunk'?

Do you place the question mark outside the quotation mark that closes the direct speech, or inside?

He then asked her, 'Do you think I'm drunk?'

> *NOTE:* The answer is that it depends on the relationship between the quotation and the sentence that contains it. The rule is — and pay attention, now!

**Punctuation Marks** (full stops, commas, question and exclamation marks, etc)
*Go inside the final quotation mark if they relate to the quoted words but outside if they relate to the whole sentence.*

In our example, the question mark relates only to the quoted statement, *Do you think I'm drunk?* and so it rightly belongs inside the final quote mark. But let's change the sentence slightly:

Should he have asked her, 'Do you think I'm drunk'?

Most punctuation marks are multi-functional and quotation marks are no exception. They can be used to indicate titles (His favourite film was the Nasir Hussains' classic, 'Phir Wohi Dil Laya Hoon'); to identify nicknames (Henry 'Rabbit Punch' Watson; Al 'Scarface' Capone); to indicate doubt, cynicism or disbelief (the hamburgers contained a mixture of liver, chicken parts and 'beef'); and to indicate that a word or phrase should not be taken literally.

## Hassles with Hyphens

The hyphen helps us construct words to help clarify meaning. At least that's what they set out to do. Take these two similar newspaper headlines:

*Man eating tiger seen near motorway*
*Man-eating tiger seen near motorway*

- The first headline suggests that a hungry gourmet has decided to barbecue some choice jungle beast near a motorway
- The second could prove fatal should you be carelessly wandering along the hard shoulder. A hyphen has made all the difference.

**Hyphens** are used to join two or more associated words. A book seller became a book-seller but is now a bookseller; life like got engaged as life-like and is now well and truly married as lifelike. Many other common words began their careers as two words linked by a hyphen: anticlimax, earring, lampshade, postgraduate, prehistoric, seaside, today washbowl.

Then there are hyphenated couples never destined to become permanent partners because of 'letter collusion' which is visually confusing: shell-like (not shelllike); semi-illiterate (not semiilliterate)— although we accept such unhyphenated words as cooperative and coordination.

Generally, hyphens are usual after the prefixes ex- (ex-cop); non- (non- starter) and self- (self-employed). They are not usually required after anti- (antifreeze); counter- (counterweight); co- (coreligionist); neo- (neoclassicism); pre(prehensile) and un-(unconditional). But there are exceptions: co-respondent (to distinguish it from a misspelt correspondent!) and re-creation (not recreation).

## A Chaos of Hyphens

Here's a handy list of words and names that are usually, but not always, hyphenated:

- anti-abortion
- bone-shaking, bull's-eye, brother-in-law, call-up, cat-o'-nine-tails, Coca-Cola, co-worker
- daddy-longlegs, daughter-in-law, deaf-and-dumb; deep-sea fishing, do-it-yourself double- cross, double-dealing, double-park, Dow-Jones
- ear-splitting, èx-husband, ex-serviceman
- face-saving, foot-and-mouth disease, forget-me-not, four-letter-word, fractions (threequarters)
- get-together, give-and-take, good-for-nothing, good-looking
- habit-forming, half-and-half half-breed (almost all words prefixed with half- carry a hyphen), helter-skelter, higgledy-piggledy high-spirited, high-tech, hit-and-run ill-advised, ill-timed, ill-treat, infra -red
- jack-o'-lantern, jiggery-pokery, Johnny-come-lately knock-for-knock, Ku -K! wc-Klan
- lady-in-waiting, large-scale, Land-River, Latter-day Saint, left-handed, light-headed, lilywhite, long-distance runner/telephone call, loose-limbed, low-key
- man-of-war, middle-aged, mother-in-law, mother-of-pearl, ne'er-do-well, non-starter
- 0-level, off-peak, off-putting, old-fashioned, one-night-stand, out-of-doors passer-by, penny-pinching, place-name, point-to-point, post-natal, pre-natal. price-fixing, pro-Irish, pro-life, etc
- quick-tempered, quick-witted right-handed, right-minded

- Set-aside, short-change, son-in-law, test-tube baby three-ring circus, tie-break, tip-off T-shirt, trap-door spider, tutti-frutti.
- tut-tut
- ultra-violet (but just as often ultraviolet) vice-presidential
- walk-on, walk-in, walkie-talkie, weather-beaten, weather-bound, well-known X-chromosone, X-ray (or x-ray)
- V-chromosome, yo-heave-ho, yo-ho-ho

## Dots, Strokes and Squiggles

The dots, strokes and squiggles may appear physically insignificant on a page of print and evanescent in our speech, but without them all would be chaos. Not knowing how to use them correctly can result in even greater chaos. If you were to say to someone:

☞ I hate habitual liars; like you, I find them detestable.

That person would very likely agree. But imagine the reaction should you monkey slightly with the punctuation:

I hate habitual liars like you; I find them detestable.

Less morbid are those grammatical gags and puzzles based on the omission of commas and other marks. The farmer raised sheep dogs and pigs (The farmer raised sheep, dogs and pigs). What is is what is not is not is it not (What is, is; what is not, is not; is it not?).

*NOTE:* You can clearly see that we need punctuation to help us express and make clear on paper what is intuitively easy with speech.

Two centuries ago, most punctuation took its cues from speech. This was a period when the predominant practice of reading aloud, with its pauses and dramatic stresses, was translated into written punctuation — rhetorical punctuation.

A hundred years on, with increased literacy, the spoken word gave way to the written. The emphasis now was on meaning rather than dramatic effect, and rhetorical (or oratorical) punctuation bowed to a more logical system. Today we have a blend of both: a system capable of conveying force, intonation, urgency, tension, doubt, rhythm and passion while never abandoning its duty to consistency and clarity of meaning.

Punctuation probably reached its zenith in the late 19th century, helping to make sense of the then fashionably interminable sentences. Sentences held together by a dozen or more commas, semicolons, brackets and other marks were commonplace. Nowadays.sentences, influenced by the brevity of newspaper style, are shorter, and the need for, the complicated division within long sentences has all but disappeared. Commas are freely dropped where the meaning remains unaffected. Stops after abbreviations are disappearing in a general quest for typographic tidiness. The majority of the English-speaking population probably goes through life without ever using, on paper, any punctuation marks other than the comma, dash and full stop.

Don't, however, be led astray by this tolerance. While parsimony in punctuation may be adequate for the majority, it will be of little use to you if you wish to raise your standards of communication. The role of punctuation in writing good English cannot be underestimated.

And take heart! Somerset Maugham couldn't handle commas. Jane Austen got her quotation marks in a twist.

George Orwell feared semicolons so much he wrote a novel without any at all. The competition isn't so awesome after all.

The marks; that help us punctuate our writing can be divided into three groups:

- UNITS OF SPACE: Sentences and paragraphs.
- DEVICES FOR SEPARATING AND JOINING: Full stops, commas, semicolons, colons, brackets, dashes and hyphens.
- SYMBOLS OF MEANING: Question and exclamation marks, quotation marks, apostrophes, strokes, asterisks, bullets, italics and underlining.

## Units of Space

Units of Space are a basic form of punctuation. They separate words, sentences and paragraphs.

Note the two groups:

## Devices for Separating and Joining

Sentences begin with a Capital letter
To help you make your writing better
Use full stops to mark the end
Of every sentence you have penned.

So runs the old schoolteachers' rhyme, and although it seems absurdly basic you'd be surprised by the number of people who either use full stops where they shouldn't or neglect to use them where they should.

### Review

Punctuation marks are symbols that indicate the structure and organization of written language. They also mark intonation and pauses to be observed when reading aloud.

In written English, punctuation is vital to disambiguate the meaning of sentences. For example, "woman, without her man, is nothing" (emphasizing the importance of men) and "woman: without her, man is nothing" (emphasizing the importance of women) have greatly different meanings, as do "eats shoots and leaves" (to mean "consumes plant growths") and "eats, shoots and leaves" (to mean "eats first, fires a weapon secondly, and leaves the scene thirdly")."King Charles walked and talked; half an hour after, his head was cut off" is less surprising than "King Charles walked and talked half an hour after his head was cut off."

The rules of punctuation vary with language, location, register and time and are constantly evolving. Certain aspects of punctuation are stylistic and are thus the author's (or editor's) choice. Tachygraphic language forms, such as those used in online chat and text messages, may have wildly different rules.

Note the relative values:

*The stop point out, with truth, the time of pause*
*A sentence doth require at ev'ry clause.*
*At ev'ry comma, stop while one you count;*
*At semicolon, two is the amount;*
*A colon doth require the time of three;*
*The period four, as learned men agree.*

The use of punctuation was not standardised until after the invention of printing. According to the 1885 edition of *The American Printer*, the importance of punctuation was noted in various sayings by children such as:

> *Charles the First walked and talked*
> *Half an hour after his head was cut off.*
> *With a semi-colon and a comma added it reads:*
> *Charles the First walked and talked;*
> *Half an hour after, his head was cut off.*

Shortly after the invention of printing, the necessity of stops or pauses in sentences for the guidance of the reader produced the colon and full point. In process of time, the comma was added, which was then merely a perpendicular line, proportioned to the body of the letter.

## Basic Rules of Punctuation

Like many of the so-called "laws" of grammar, the rules for using punctuation are conventions that have changed over the centuries. They vary across national boundaries (American punctuation, differs from British practice) and even from one writer to the next.

Until the 18th century, punctuation was primarily related to spoken delivery (elocution); the marks were interpreted as pauses that could be counted out: "A Comma stops the Voice while we may privately tell one, a Semi-colon two; a Colon three; and a Period four." This declamatory basis for punctuation gradually gave way to the syntactic approach used today.

Understanding the principles behind the common marks of punctuation should strengthen your understanding of grammar and help you to use the marks consistently in your own writing. Punctuation has the primary responsibility of contributing to the plainness of one's meaning. It has the secondary responsibility of being as invisible as possible, of not calling attention to itself.

## The most common marks of punctuation:

☞ Periods                        ☞ Question marks
☞ Exclamation points             ☞ Commas
☞ Semicolons                     ☞ Colons
☞ Dashes                         ☞ Apostrophes
☞ Quotation marks.

## End Punctuation:

☞ Periods
☞ Question Marks
☞ Exclamation Points

## There are only three ways to end a sentence:

☞ a period (.)
☞ a question mark (?)
☞ an exclamation point (!).

**PERIOD:** The Americans call it a PERIOD; the British a full-stop.

Until the 20th century, the question mark was more commonly known as a point of interrogation.

The exclamation point has been used since the 17th century to indicate strong emotion, such as surprise, wonder, disbelief, or pain.

Punctuation marks are the **road signs** placed along the highway of our communication—to control speeds, provide directions, and prevent head-on collisions.

*A period has the unblinking finality of a red light*
*The comma is a flashing yellow light that asks us only to slow down*
*The semicolon is a stop sign that tells us to ease gradually to a halt, before gradually starting up again.*

Odds are that you probably already recognise the road signs of punctuation, though now and then you might get the signs confused.

*The best way to understand punctuation is to study the sentence structures that the marks accompany.*

## End Punctuation

☞ A sentence may end with
☞ a period (.)
☞ a question mark (?)\
☞ an exclamation point (!).

*Use a period at the end of a sentence that makes a statement:*

*I was eleven years old. And when I was strong enough, I dedicated my life to the study of fencing. So the next time we meet, I will not fail. I will go up to the six-fingered man and say, "Hello. My name is Imtiaz. You killed my father. Prepare to die."*

*Notice that a period goes inside a closing quotation mark*

<u>*Use a question mark after direct questions, as in this exchange:*</u>

The Grandson: Is this a mischief book?
Grandpa: Wait, just wait.
The Grandson: Well, when does it get good?
Grandpa: Keep your shirt on, and let me read.

*However, at the end of indirect quotations (that is, reporting someone else's question in our own words), use a period instead of a question mark:*

☞ The boy asked if there was mischief in the book.

Now and then we may use an exclamation point at the end of a sentence to express strong emotion:

*You only think I guessed wrong! That's what's so funny! I switched glasses when your back was turned! Ha ha! You fool! Ha ha ha ha ha ha ha! Ha ha ha ha ha ha ha!*

This is an extreme use of exclamations. In our own writing, we should be careful not to deaden the effect of the exclamation point by overworking it.

*Take the three end marks of punctuation: periods, question marks, and exclamation points.* They not only put the brakes on a sentence but also suggest its tone.

**Marks of punctuation:**
☞ Apostrophes
☞ Asterisks
☞ Brackets
☞ Bullets
☞ Colons
☞ Commas

☞ Dashes
☞ Diacritic marks
☞ Ellipsis
☞ Exclamation points
☞ Hyphens
☞ Parentheses
☞ Periods
☞ Question marks
☞ Quotation marks
☞ Semicolons
☞ Slashes
☞ Spacing
☞ Strike-throughs.

**Emoticons,** the smiling, winking and frowning faces that inhabit the computer keyboard, have not only hung around long past their youth faddishness of the 1990s, but they have grown up. Twenty-five years after they were invented as a form of computer-geek shorthand, emoticons—an open-source form of pop art that has evolved into a quasi-accepted form of punctuation—are now indispensable for some.

There was a time, of course, that emoticons seemed intrinsically youthful.

But after 25 years of use, emoticons have started to jump off the page and into our spoken language.

Though we think of emoticons, or 'smileys,' as an Internet-era phenomenon, their earliest ancestors were created on typewriters. In 1912, the writer Ambrose Bierce proposed a new punctuation device called a 'snigger point,' a smiling face represented by \__/!, to connote jocularity.

The apostrophe may be the simplest and yet most frequently misused mark of punctuation in English.

*Six guidelines for using the mark correctly*

## 1. Use an Apostrophe to show the Omission of Letters in a Contraction

*Use the apostrophe to form contractions:*
  I'm (I am)
  You're (you are)
  He's (he is)
  She's (she is)
  It's (it is)
  We're (we are)
  They're (they are)
  Isn't (is not)
  Aren't (are not)
  Can't (cannot)
  Don't (do not)
  Who's (who is)
  Won't (will not)

Be careful to place the apostrophe where the letter or letters have been omitted, which is not always the same place where the two words have been joined.

*NOTE:* Don't confuse the contraction it's (meaning, "it is") with the possessive pronoun its:
• It's the first day of spring.
• Our bird has escaped from its cage.

## 2. Use an Apostrophe with -s for Possessives of Singular Nouns

Use an apostrophe plus -s to show the possessive form of a singular noun, even if that singular noun already ends in -s:

> Hemant's crayon
> My daughter's first day at school
> Wordsworth's poetry
> Dylan Thomas's poetry
> Today's weather report
> The boss's problem
> Star Jones's talk show
> Victoria Beckham's husband

## 3. Use an Apostrophe without -s for Possessives of Most Plural Nouns

To form the possessive of a plural noun that already ends in -s, add an apostrophe:

> the girls' swing set (the swing set belonging to the girls)
> the students' projects (the projects belonging to the students)
> the Johnsons' house (the house belonging to the Johnsons)
> If the plural noun does not end in -s, add an apostrophe plus -s:
> the women's conference (the conference belonging to the women)
> the children's toys (the toys belonging to the children)
> the men's training camp (the training camp belonging to the men)

## 4. Use an Apostrophe with -s When Two or More Nouns Possess the Same Thing

When two or more nouns possess the same thing, add an apostrophe plus -s to the last noun listed:

Ben and Jerry's Magic Show

Meera and Nishi's school project (Meera and Nishi
worked together on the same project)

*When two or more nouns separately possess*
something, add an *apostrophe to each* noun listed:

Tim's and Mukesh's ice cream (Each boy has his own
ice cream.)

Meera and Nishi's school projects (Each girl has her
own project.)

**5. Do Not Use an Apostrophe with Possessive Pronouns**
Because possessive pronouns already show ownership, it's*
not necessary to add an apostrophe:

| | |
|---|---|
| yours | his |
| hers | its* |
| ours | theirs |

However, *we do add an apostrophe* plus -s to form the
possessive of some indefinite pronouns:

anybody's guess
one's personal responsibility
somebody's wallet

* *Don't confuse the contraction it's* (meaning, "it is") *with
the possessive* pronoun its:
*It's the first day of spring.*
*Our bird has escaped from its cage.*

**6. Generally, Do Not Use an Apostrophe to Form a Plural**
As a general rule, use only an -s (or an -es) without an
apostrophe to form the plurals of nouns—including dates,
acronyms, and family names:

Markets were booming in the 1990s.
The tax advantages offered by India make them
attractive investments.
The T-Series have sold all of their CDs.

To avoid confusion, we may occasionally need to use apostrophes to indicate the plural forms of certain letters and expressions that are not commonly found in the plural:

☞ Mind your p's and q's.

Let's **accept the proposal** without any **if's, and's**, or *but's*.

The comma, says the **Time** magazine article, can be compared to "a flashing yellow light that asks us only to slow down." But when do we need to flash that light, and when is it better to let the sentence ride on through without interruption?

**The four main guidelines for using commas effectively:**

**1. Use a Comma before a Coordinator**
Use a comma before a coordinator (*and, but, yet, or, nor, for, so*) that links two main clauses:

☞ "The optimist thinks that this is the best of all possible worlds, and the pessimist knows it."
(Robert Oppenheimer)
☞ "You may be disappointed if you fail, but you are doomed if you don't try."
(Beverly Sills)

*NOTE:* However, do not use a comma before a coordinator that links two words or phrases:

"Jatin and Dimple sang and danced all night."

**2. Use a Comma to Separate Items in a Series**
Use a comma between words, phrases, or clauses that appear in a series of three or more:

☞ "You get injected, inspected, detected, infected, neglected, and selected."

*"It is by the goodness of God that in our country we have three unspeakably precious things: freedom of speech, freedom of conscience, and the prudence never to practice either of them."*
(Mark Twain)

> *NOTE:* In each example a comma appears before but not after the coordinator.

### 3. Use a Comma after an Introductory Word Group
Use a comma after a phrase or clause that precedes the subject of the sentence:

☞ "When you get to the end of your rope, tie a knot and hang on."
(Franklin Roosevelt)

☞ "If at first you don't succeed, failure may be your style."
(Quentin Crisp)

However, if there's no danger of confusing readers, you may omit the comma after a short introductory phrase:

"At first I thought the challenge was staying awake, so I ate 10 burges and 20-ounce Mountain Dews."

### 4. Use a Pair of Commas to set of Interruptions
Use a pair of commas to set off words, phrases, or clauses that interrupt a sentence:

☞ "Words are, of course, the most powerful drug used by mankind."

(Rudyard Kipling)

But don't use commas to set off words that directly affect the essential meaning of the sentence:

☞ "Your manuscript is both good and original. But the part that is good is not original, and the part that is original is not good."
(Samuel Johnson)

**Quotation marks,** sometimes referred to as quotes or inverted commas, are punctuation marks used in pairs to set off a quotation or a piece of dialogue.

## Five guidelines for using quotation marks effectively

### 1. Direct Quotations

Use double quotation marks (" ") to enclose a direct quotation:

After telling an audience that young people today "think work is a four-letter word," Senator Hillary Rodham Clinton said she apologised to her daughter.

"No good deed," wrote Clare Booth Luce, "will go unpunished."

> *NOTE:* Direct quotations repeat a speaker's exact words.
> In contrast, indirect quotations are summaries or paraphrases of someone else's words. Do not use quotation marks around indirect quotations:
>
> ✘  Paul said, "I'm satisfied."
> ✓  Paul said that he was satisfied.

### 2. Titles

Use double quotation marks to enclose the titles of songs, short stories, essays, poems, and articles:

Do not put quotation marks around the titles of books, newspapers, or magazines; instead, *italicize* or *underline* those titles.

### 3. Quotations within Quotations

Use a pair of single quotation marks (' ') to enclose a title, direct quotation, or piece of dialogue that appears within another quotation:

Julie once said, "I have never read much poetry, but I love the sonnet 'To India My Native Land.'"

Notice that two separate quotation marks appear at the end of the sentence: a single mark to close the title and a double mark to close the direct quotation.

### 4. Commas and Quotation Marks

When a comma or a period appears at the end of a quotation, put it inside the quotation mark:

"Gluttony is an emotional disease," he once wrote, "a sign that something is eating us."

### 5. Other Marks of Punctuation with Quotation Marks

When a semicolon or a colon appears at the end of a quotation, put it outside the quotation mark:

John Wayne never said, "A man's gotta do what a man's gotta do"; however, he did say, "A man ought to do what's right."

When a question mark or an exclamation point appears at the end of a quotation, put it inside the quotation mark if it belongs to the quotation:

He sang, "How Can I Miss You
If You Don't Go Away?"

But if the question mark or exclamation point does not belong to the quotation itself, put it outside the quotation mark:

Did Madonna really sing, "His Heart Was Pure"?

## 10 Rules Of Punctuation

While there are no hard and fast rules about punctuation, there are good style guidelines. This is a list of our **ten most commonly used punctuation marks and a guide to their use.**

### 10. Comma

Use commas to separate independent clauses in a sentence, for example:
☞ The game was over, but the crowd refused to leave.
☞ Yesterday was her brother's birthday, so she took him out to dinner.

Use commas after introductory words, phrases, or clauses that come before the main clause:
☞ While I was eating, the cat scratched at the door.
☞ If you are ill, you ought to see a doctor.

> *NOTE:* You should not do the reverse of this. For example, the following two cases are wrong:
> ✘ The cat scratched at the door, while I was eating.
> ✔ You ought to see a doctor, if you are ill.

Introductory words that should be followed by a comma are: *yes, however, and well.*

*For Example:*
☞ Yes, you can come to the party

*Use a pair of commas to separate an aside from the main body of the sentence.* For example:
☞ Jugal and Pinky, the couple from next door, are coming for dinner tonight.

*NOTE:* You can test this by removing the aside from the sentence. If the sentence still reads correctly, you have probably used the commas as you should. In the case above, this would render: Jugal and Pinky are coming for dinner tonight.

*Do not use commas to separate essential elements of the sentence.* For example:
- ✓ Students who cheat only harm themselves.
- ✗ The baby wearing a yellow dress is my niece.

## The Oxford Comma

It is also known as the **Serial Comma** or the **Harvard Comma.** The Oxford comma is much more widespread in American English than British English. When using the Oxford comma, all items in a list of three or more items are separated.

*For Example:*
☞ I love apples, pears, and oranges.

*NOTE:* Note the comma after "pears". Many people prefer not to use this style and will omit the final comma. *This is called the Oxford comma because it is the standard method taught at Oxford University.*

Use commas to set off all *geographical names,items in date's* (except the month and day), *addresses (except the street number and name), and titles in names.*

N.E. Manipur in the North-East, gets its name from Land of Gems, India.

July 13, 1963, was a momentous day in his life.

Occasionally, you will see a comma between a house

number and street. This is not wrong, it is just old fashioned. It is not done in modern times, however.

**Use a comma to shift between the main discourse and a quotation.**

☞ Jetender said without emotion, "I'll see you tomorrow."

☞ "I was able," she answered, "to complete the assignment."

Use commas if they prevent confusion:

☞ To George, Harrison had been a sort of idol.

## 9. Period or Full Stop

The primary use of a period is to end a sentence. Its second important use is for abbreviations. There are stylistic differences here.

> *NOTE:* Martin Fowler, author of *Modern English Usage*, says that we should place a period at the end of an abbreviation only when the final letter of the abbreviation is not the final letter of the expanded word.

*For example:*

Jesus Christ was born c. 4-6AD

The abbreviation is for the word "circa" – as it ends in an 'a' and the abbreviation is normally 'c' – we include the period.

☞ Mr James was happy to see his wife

☞ St Patrick lived in Ireland

In the first case above, "Mr" is an abbreviation for mister. Because mister ends in an 'r' and the abbreviation includes that 'r', we omit the period.

**Other**

The other use of the period for abbreviations is to always

include the period, regardless of whether the final letter is included.

Mr. Jones was happy to see his wife

*If an abbreviated phrase is pronounced, we do not include periods.* For example:

☞ NASA is correct, N.A.S.A is incorrect. In some cases the periods are omitted even when the word is not pronounced, usually because it is a very commonly known term. For example: BHU (Banaras Hindu University, Varanasi).

In the case of a word like et cetera (etc.,) we always include the period.

## 8. Question Mark

The question mark is a fairly easy punctuation mark to use. It has one use, and one use alone. It goes at the end of a sentence which is a question. For example:

☞ How many will be at the party?

*NOTE:* Do not include a period when using a question mark.

Do not use a combination of question marks and exclamation marks in formal writing, though this is gaining acceptance in informal writing – particularly on the internet.

One thing to be careful of is to not include a question mark when it is not needed:

✘ I wonder how many people will come to the party?

While you are expressing a thought that seems to require an answer, you are doing so with a statement. This is the most common mistake made when using a question mark.

## 7. Exclamation Mark

Only use this when issuing a command or speaking forcefully! As in the case of the question mark, do not follow this with a period and do not combine it with other punctuation marks.

Oh, and only one is needed. Two or three exclamation marks in a row is completely unnecessary.

## 6. Quote Marks

Quotation marks are used to quote another person's words exactly, whether they be spoken, or written. For example:

☞ The housemaster said, "We are going shopping." – note the capitalization of "We". You should do this unless you are quoting in a run-on sentence:

The housemaster said "we are going shopping" because they had no milk. Note the omission of the comma in this case also.

If you are quoting a person who is quoting another person, use a single quotation mark like this:

John said, "My neighbour yelled at me today! He said 'get off my lawn!'"

When introducing a quotation after an independent clause, use a colon and not a comma to begin:

The Professor explains, "The gestures used for greeting others differ greatly from one culture to another." (Not an independent clause)

Professor explains cultural differences in greeting customs: "Touching is not a universal sign of greeting. (This is an independent clause)

*Quotation marks can also be used to denote irony or sarcasm, or to note something unusual about it:*

The great march of "progress" has left millions impoverished and hungry.

## Punctuation with quotations

Punctuation that belongs to the original quote should be inside the quote marks. Punctuation relating to the entire sentence should be outside.

Philip asked, "Do you need this book?"

Does Dr. Sharma always say to her students, "You must work harder"?

Always *put colons and semicolons* outside quotes. Put commas *and periods* inside quotations unless followed by *parenthesis*:

He said, "I may forget your name, but I never remember a face."

## 5. Colon

A colon should be used after a complete statement in order to introduce one or more directly related ideas, such as a series of directions, a list, or a quotation or other comment illustrating or explaining the statement. For example:

☞ The daily newspaper contains four sections: news, sports, entertainment, and classified ads.

The colon is also used to separate chapter and verse from the Bible (I Corinthians 12:30), to separate hours, minutes, and seconds: 13:49:08, and as eyeballs in smiley faces.

## 4. Semicolon

• Use a semicolon to join related independent clauses in compound sentences. For example:

☞ Jim worked hard to earn his degree; consequently, he was certain to achieve a distinction.

☞ Lalita overslept by three hours; she was going to be late for work again.

*The semicolon is also used to separate items in a series if the elements of the series already include commas.* For example:

☞ Members of the band include Harish, sitarist; Tarun, tabla player; and Sapan Ganguly, trumpeter.

### 3. Apostrophe

The apostrophe has three uses:
(1)  To form possessives of nouns
(2)  To show the omission of letters
(3)  To indicate certain plurals of lowercase letters.

**Forming possessives**
☞ the boy's bat
☞ three day's journey

*If the noun after "of" is a building, an object, or a piece of furniture, then no apostrophe is needed.* For example:
☞ The car door.

**Showing omission**
☞ He'll go = He will go
☞ Could've = could have (Not "could of"!)

**Forming plurals**
Apostrophes are used to form plurals of letters that appear in lower case. For example:
☞ Mind your p's and q's

### 2. Parentheses

*Parentheses are occasionally and sparingly used for extra, nonessential material included in a sentence.* For example:

*dates, sources, or ideas that are subordinate or tangential to the rest of the sentence are set apart in parentheses.*

**Parentheses always appear in pairs.**

☞ Before arriving at the station, the old train caught fire.

## 1. Dash or Hyphen

*Dash*

Use the dash for emphasis to a point or to set off an explanatory comment; *but don't overuse dashes, or they will lose their impact.*

A dash is typically represented on a computer by two hyphens with no spaces before, after, or between the hyphens.

☞ To some of you, my proposals may seem radical–even revolutionary.

It is also used for an appositive phrase that already includes commas.

The boys–Joshi, Jugal, and Jogi–left the party early.

> *NOTE:* As you can see, the dash can be used in the same way as parentheses.

*Hyphen*

Use a hyphen to join two or more words serving as a single adjective before a noun:

☞ chocolate-covered peanuts

*Don't use the hyphen when the noun comes first:*

The peanuts are chocolate covered.

*Use a hyphen with compound numbers:*

☞ Forty-five

*You should also use a hyphen to avoid confusion in a sentence:*
☞ He had to re-sign the contract
☞ He had to resign his job

*Use a hyphen with the prefixes ex- (meaning former), self-, all-; with the suffix -elect; between a prefix and a capitalized word; and with figures or letters:*

| | |
|---|---|
| ☞ ex-husband | ☞ self-assured |
| ☞ mid-August | ☞ all-inclusive |
| ☞ president-elect | ☞ anti-Indian |
| ☞ T-shirt | ☞ pre-Independence |
| ☞ mid-1990s | ☞ self-employed |

## The Full Stop

*'Punctuation is. . . not a fireworks display to show off your dashes and gaspers. Remember the first rule: the best punctuation is the full stop.'*

•     The full stop (or stop, point or period) is the most emphatic, abrupt and unambiguous of all the punctuation marks.
• It is used like a knife to cut off a sentence at the required length.
• The rule is that simple: where you place your stop is up to you, but generally it is at the point where a thought is complete.
• When you are about to embark on another thought, that's the time to think about a full stop. Master this principle and you can then move on to using full stops *stylistically*, for emphasis:
*You couldn't get near Harish all day because he was constantly on the prowl, hunched in his greasy pants and*

*dirty sweater, looking mean and taciturn and with his mind no doubt churning with murderous thoughts, for he had announced to too many people in too many places and in too loud a voice that he would kill Minu the instant he clapped eyes on him. And he did.*

That delayed full stop, preceded by mounting tension and followed by the shock conclusion delivered in just three words, helps to convey an almost casual callousness. The two stops serve their purpose perfectly; they make the reader stop and reflect.

Here's another passage, this time displaying a variety of punctuation marks. The full stop, however, is easily the most predominant:

*With intense frustration, Goel grabbed the man, surprising him. 'No you don't!' he yelled hoarsely.*

*The man recovered, fighting back. Fiercely. Savagely. Hard breathing. Curses. Grunts. An alarming stream of crimson from Goel's left eye. Pulses racing, they glared at one another, each daring the other to make a move. A car horn in the distance. Shouts.*

That's highly stylised prose, and could be criticised for its over-use of sentence fragments rather than complete sentences.

Full stops control the length of your sentences, so remember:

☞ Try to keep sentences variable in length, but generally short.

☞ Using long sentences doesn't necessarily make you a better writer.

## Full Stops and Abbreviations

Full stops have also been used traditionally to shorten words, names and phrases. The convention was to use full stops for chopped-off words, or abbreviations:

| | |
|---|---|
| • doz. | • Sat. |
| • Oct. | • Prof. |
| • Staffs. | • lab. |
| • Inst. | • Appt. |

Do not shorten if the first and last letters of the word, or contractions:

| | |
|---|---|
| • Mr Dr | • gdn |
| • mfr | • St |
| • yd | • Revd |

*NOTE:* Thus, by the rules *per cent* was considered to be an abbreviation because it chopped off the 'urn' from per cen turn. And while the Rev. Peter required a full stop, the Revd Peter didn't.

The stops are being abandoned in favour of speed, economy and cleaner typography. You will still see stops used for both abbreviations and contractions and sometimes to avoid ambiguity. Here is a sampling of the new order:

| Formerly | Now (mostly) |
|---|---|
| 6 a.m. | 6am |
| e.g. | eg |
| 1472 A.D. | 1472 AD |
| 16 Jan. | 16 Jan |
| Wm. Shakespeare | Wm Shakespeare |

| | |
|---|---|
| viz. | viz |
| R.S.V.P. | RSVP |
| U.K | UK |

*Full stops are still required for certain other functional expressions:*

For money units: ₹9.99, $99.89

For decimals: 20.86, 33.33%

For time (hours and minutes): 11.45am, 23.45 hrs

## The Comma

The comma is the most flexible and most versatile of all the punctuation marks. And because it is also the least emphatic mark it is also the most complex and subtle.

A lot of the trouble with commas arises because many people seem to think of them as indicating 'breath pauses'. That may have been the case when the language was more orally inclined, and in much early prose it is common to find commas following speech patterns. *Today*, however, the placement of *commas* invariably follows grammatical logic rather than *indicating* rhetorical pauses:

Every year over the British Isles, half a million meteorites enter the atmosphere.

Most writing today requires commas that serve a logical purpose, usually to separate different thoughts or nuances of thought within sentences:

☞ The snapshot with its naively honest images revolutionised our way of seeing the world.

## Functions of the Comma

### SETTING APART NAMES AND PERSONS
☞ Are you meeting him tomorrow, John? Listen, Joyce, I've had enough. And that, ladies and gentlemen, is that.

### ITEMISING WORDS
☞ Please place all towels, costumes, clothing and valuables in the lockers provided.

### ITEMISING WORD GROUPS
☞ Please place any articles of clothing, swimming and sporting equipment, personal belongings, but not money and jewellery, in the lockers.

### ENCLOSING ADDITIONAL THOUGHTS OR QUALIFICATIONS
☞ The occasion was, on the whole, conducted with considerable dignity. The judges thought it was, arguably, one of his finest novels.

### SETTING APART INTERJECTIONS
☞ Look, I've had enough! Blimey, isn't the beach crowded!

### BEFORE DIRECT SPEECH
☞ Jill turned abruptly and said, 'if that's the way you feel, then go home!'

### INTRODUCING QUESTIONS
☞ You'll be going soon, won't you? She's marrying James tomorrow, isn't she?

### EMPHASISING POINTS OF VIEW
☞ Naturally, I'll look after the car. Of course, she fully deserves it.

## SETTING OFF COMPARATIVE OR CONTRASTING STATEMENTS
☞ The taller they are, the farther they fall.
☞ The more he said he adored her, the less she cared.

## REINFORCING STATEMENTS
☞ She's ill because she won't eat, that's why!
☞ It'll come right in the end, I'm sure.

## AFTER INTRODUCTORY WORDS
☞ Wafer chips, which are far from fat-free, pose a problem for dieters.

Omitting the opening comma required to separate a subordinate clause (which are far from fat-free) from the main clause (Wafer chips. . . pose a problem for dieters) is a common mistake and one that usually leads to ambiguity. With the commas correctly in place, as in our example, we are in no doubt that the description 'far from fat-free' applies to all sausages. But omit that opening comma and a different meaning can be conveyed: Sausages which are far from fat-free, pose a problem for dieters.

Now the statement is saying that only those wafer chips that are 'far from fat- free' are a problem. But if that is what is actually meant, the remaining comma is redundant.

*Here's another example:*
Overnight fans had painted messages on the road outside his home 'We love you Rajesh Khanna'.

> *NOTE:* Overnight fans? Are these a different breed from ordinary fans? Obviously a comma after the separate thought 'Overnight' is required to make things clear.

*Using commas appropriately also includes not over-using them:*

It is, curiously, surprising when, say, you hear your name announced in a foreign language, or even in a strange accent.

Although grammatically correct that sentence seems to be hedged with *ifs, buts, maybes* and *pontifications*. Can it be rewritten in a more direct style, while still conveying the several shades of meaning?

Curiously, it is surprising when, for example, you hear your name announced in a foreign language or even in a strange accent.

The sentence, less two commas, is now a little more direct.

Here's another example of 'comma bloat' which can be rewritten without using any commas at all.

Mr Bhattacharya had not, previously, met the plaintiff except when, in 1974, he had, unexpectedly, found himself in Delhi.

It's worth looking a little closer at comma-reduction. Take this simple sentence:

A. My hobby, trainspotting, is, to many, a bit of a joke.

B. My hobby, trainspotting, is to many, a bit of a joke.

C. My hobby, trains potting, is to many a bit of a joke.

D. My hobby trainspotting, is to many a bit of a joke.

E. My hobby trainspotting is to many a bit of a joke.

*Pedants might claim that all these sentences differ in nuances of meaning, but to the average reader they all mean the same thing. So we are left with choosing which one we would use to express our thought clearly, economically and elegantly.*

To some extent the apt use of commas is an acquired skill — but certainly one worth pursuing. Merely scanning a sentence for sense and clarity will usually tell you.

*Using Commas with Adjectives*

See if you can work out, in these two sentences, why one has the adjectives separated by commas, and the other does not:

☞ The night resounded with a loud, chilling, persistent ringing.

☞ It was a large brick Victorian mansion.

The reasons are embodied in two seemingly simple rules worth remembering:

- Where the adjectives (or other modifiers) define separate attributes (loud, chilling, persistent), they are best separated by commas.
- Where the adjectives work together to create a single image (large, brick, Victorian), the commas are best omitted.

Two seemingly simple rules, but they can be tricky to apply. Sometimes you may be led into ambiguity and have to resort to common sense:

- Myra was a pretty smart young woman.
- Myra was a pretty, smart young woman.

Well, does the writer mean that Myra was pretty and smart, or just very smart?

## Using Commas with Adverbs and Adverbial Phrases

It is customary to use commas to enclose modifying adverbs and adverbial phrases such as *however, indeed, nevertheless, in fact, needless to say, no doubt, incidentally, anyway, for example, on the contrary, of course* and *as we have seen:*

You are, nevertheless, guilty the first charge.

Increasingly, however, [notice the enclosing commas!] such commas are dropped when the meaning remains clear without them:

You are nevertheless guilty of the first charge.

But be alert for ambiguity:

The hospital informed us that both victims were, happily, recovering.

Remove the enclosing commas either side of happily and you'd give the impression that the victims were not only recovering but having the time of their lives!

## Commas are also needed for sentences beginning with adverbs:

* Curiously, the two cousins had never met.
* Ironically, they discovered they were sisters.
* Looking scared, Peter peered out of the window.

### *Also for sentences containing adverbial clauses:*

Peter, not usually given to heroics, smartly lowered his head.

## Using Commas to Parenthesise

One of the most interesting, but also perhaps the most contentious, uses of commas is to parenthesise (or bracket) relevant but not essential matter from the main part of the sentence:

The wild hyacinths (which are now at the height of their season) tint the woods with a pale blue mist.

The essential message here is *The wild hyacinths tint the woods with a pale blue mist.* But then we've had a further thought — which are now at the height of their season — which we'd like to include in the same sentence. Sometimes we enclose such additions in parentheses (brackets) as above, but mostly we use a pair of far convenient and less disruptive commas:

The wild hyacinths, which are now at the height of their season, tint the woods with a pale blue mist.

Now that we've seen how commas are used to isolate subordinate statements, what are these two commas doing in this sentence?

The two lead actors, who appear in 'Grease', won their respective roles after many gruelling years in musicals.

The two enclosing commas here are telling 'us that who appear in 'Deewar' is non-essential information. But if you -rewrite the sentence without that phrase it doesn't make sense: we don't know who the lead actors are or what they are doing.

In fact who appear in 'Deewar' is a defining or restrictive phrase — one that identifies, modifies or qualifies its subject. It is essential, not non-essential, information. So the sentence should read:

The two lead actors who appear in 'Deewar' won their respective roles after many gruelling years films.

**To summarise:**

- Where a phrase or clause does not define or qualify the subject, indicate that it is non-essential matter by isolating it with a pair of commas.
- Where a phrase or clause defines or qualifies the subject, weld it to, the subject by omitting the commas.

## The Semicolon

There is something about semicolons that can raise the blood pressure. The writer George Orwell was so against them that he wrote one of his novels, Coming Up For Air (1939), without a single semicolon in it. Actually, three crept in, only to be removed in later editions.

George Bernard Shaw complained of T. E. Lawrence that while he threw colons about like a madman he hardly used semicolons at all.

More recently, Martin Amis, in his novel *Money,* reportedly used just one.

*A semicolon is a pause somewhere between a strong comma and a weak full stop.* And despite its dismissal by many writers and teachers it has a number of practical grammatical and stylistic functions:

• To join words, word groups and sentences. Occasionally we find ourselves writing a long sentence with too many connecting words such as and, but and also, with the danger of getting into an impossible tangle:

The history of the semicolon and colon is one of confusion because there are no precise rules governing their use and, furthermore, many writers would argue that both marks are really stylistic rather than parenthetical devices, and can in any case be easily replaced by commas, stops and dashes, and there the argument rests.

There's nothing grammatically wrong with that, but it is unwieldy and unappealing to both eye and mind. Many writers would, without hesitation, recast it as two or more separate sentences:

Judicious use of full stops to achieve shorter sentences can aid understanding, and that is certainly the case here. But some writers, feeling that the original long sentence is, after all, about a single subject and should therefore be kept as a whole and not split apart, would turn to the semicolon to achieve unity of thought without making things hard for the reader:

To separate word groups already containing commas. Any sentence that is essentially a list should be crystal clear and easily read. Most 'sentence lists' adequately separate the items with commas, but sometimes the items themselves are groups containing commas and require semicolons for clarity. These two examples illustrate just how handy semicolons can be:

Those present included Mr and Mrs Allison, their daughters Sarah, Megan and Sue; the Smith twins; Reg and Paul Watson; Joyce, Helen and Bill Hobson; etc.

## To provide pauses before certain adverbs:

There are certain adverbs and conjunctions that require a preceding pause, but one longer and stronger than that provided by a comma. Look at this example:

**With a comma:**
It was a beautiful car, moreover it was economical to run.

**With a semicolon:**
It was a beautiful car; moreover it was economical to run.

You can see and hear that need for a substantial pause before moreover, can't you?

A comma is wrong on both grammatical and rhetorical counts. Here's another example; read it and note your instinctive pause before nevertheless:

- Joe claimed he'd beaten the bookies on every race; nevertheless he was broke as usual when he left the track.

Watch out for therefore, however, besides, also, moreover, furthermore, hence, consequently and subsequently; in many constructions they will require a preceding semicolon.

- To induce a mild shock or make a joke. Semicolons can help the writer emphasise contrast and incongruity. For a woman to remark. I thought his wife was lovely but that her dress was in poor taste.

This would be certainly lacking in feminine acuity. Here's what she might wish she'd said with the use of a mental semicolon:

- I loved his wife; pity about the frock.

A semicolon is adroitly used by Henry Thoreau in *Walden*, although in a more self-deprecating vein:

I had more visitors while I lived in the woods than at any other period in my life; I mean that I had some.

## The Colon

The legendary grammarian Henry Fowler defined the function of the colon as 'delivering the goods that have been invoiced in the preceding words'. More matter-of-factly, the colon acts as a pointing finger, as if to warn the reader about a statement ahead:

'Wait for it. . . here it comes!'

Although under threat from the dash, the colon is a versatile workhorse, and many colon-scoffers are silenced when confronted with the range of its functions:

• *To introduce a list.* This is probably how colons are most commonly used:

☞ Detective Stevens entered and took it all in: the body, the still smouldering mattress, the cigarette butts on the floor.

## • To present a conclusion

☞ There was one very obvious reason for Ernest's failure to keep the job: his right hand never knew what his left was doing.

• To present an explanation or example.

☞ There are three reasons why Akasa near Defence Colony is an outstanding restaurant: excellent cuisine, beautifully restored interiors, and super-attentive staff

• To introduce a quotation or indirect speech.

☞ Gradually, one by one, the words came back to me: 'And we forget because we must and not because we will.'

The Minister strode to the platform, opened his notes and glared at the assembly:

☞ 'You have not come here for nothing,' he growled.

• *As a substitute for a conjunction.* In this example, the writer preferred the punchier colon to a choice of conjunctions such as and or but:

☞ Ranjit felled him with a dazzling left hook that came out of nowhere: Hayman did not get up.

• To introduce questions.

☞ The essential issue is simply this: did she or did she not seduce Sir Timothy in the stable block?

• To introduce subtitles.

☞ Gilbert White: Observer in God's Little Acre.

☞ Men at War: An introduction to Chess.

- *To link contrasting statements.* In this role the colon shares with the semicolon the ability to administer surprise and shock. The choice is a matter of taste:

☞ Her love affair with her son's school, its history, its achievements, its famous alumni and its crumbling charm would have endured for ever but for one minor consideration: the ₹12,000 monthly fees.

- Other sundry uses.

If you ever read a stageplay, you'll often find it laid out something like this:

GEORGE: You've said enough —

ANNA: I haven't even started!

GEORGE: Enough! D'you hear me!

*Then there is the 'biblical' colon, separating chapter and verse* (Ecclesiastes 3:12); *the mathematical colon used to express ratios* (Male athletes outnumber females by 3:2); *and the time colon* (The train departs at 12:45).

In the USA it is customary to use colons to open a letter:

*NOTE:* Dear Anna: I do look forward to seeing you soon.

*NOTE: The difference between a colon and a semicolon is not a difference in weight or force; the two marks are mostly used for quite different purposes.*

— Except in the case of introducing subtitles (see above), a colon is not followed by a capital letter unless the word is a proper noun; Emma, Ford Motor Co, etc.
— Don't use colons where they are not needed, as in:
✖ The man was amazing and was able to play: the piano, violin, double bass, trombone, clarinet, harp and drums. The colon is clearly redundant.

## Brackets and Parentheses

Parenthesised (the term parenthesis, via Latin and Greek, means 'an insertion besides') by enclosing it between two commas.

The bracket's embrace extremely adaptable, as the following catalogue of examples of usage will demonstrate:

- ADDING INFORMATION — One of the earliest dictionaries is that of Oxford
- OFFERING EXPLANATION — Unable to follow the instructions in French and after nothing but trouble she returned the car to the garage.
- AFTERTHOUGHT — Travel by car, choose the cross-channel route that offers best value for money, and look out for bargains.
- CLARIFICATION — The directive stated quite clearly that the department would be closed from March 1.

| | |
|---|---|
| • COMMENT | Cruelty to animals (I noted a scene in which a donkey's tail was lied to a post, and another where a tin can with a lit firecracker in it was attached to a dog's tail) was a fairly common sight in children's comic papers in the 1920s. |
| • ILLUSTRATION | The candidate spent far too long discussing irrelevancies (20 minutes on the price of footwear; another ten on tax havens) with the inevitable result that most of us walked out. |
| • TO EXPRESS AN ASIDE | She claims to be 35. |
| • TO INDICATE OPTIONS | Your document(s) will be returned in due course. |

There is an important grammatical difference between parenthesising material within commas and within brackets. Generally, material enclosed by commas is still very much part of the sentence and should observe the grammatical conventions of that sentence. Bracketed material, on the other hand, is rather more distanced from the sentence into which it is inserted, and can assume its own punctuation.

## The Square Bracket

The square bracket has an entirely different function from that of parentheses: words enclosed within them are not intended to be part of a sentence, but as an editorial or authorial interjection:

☞ It was a matter of opinion that if offered the position, he [Professor Kapil Kapoor] would most likely refuse it on moral grounds.

*That sentence came at the end of a very long paragraph; the professor's name had been mentioned at the beginning, but other names and much discussion followed so that the late reference to he was in danger of being misunderstood. The editor therefore inserted the name [Professor Professor Kapil Kapoor] in square brackets as a reminder and also to indicate that the intervention was the editor's and not the author's.*

One of the most common uses of square brackets is to enclose the adverb sic (from the Latin *sicut*, meaning 'just as') to indicate that incorrect or doubtful matter is quoted exactly from the original.

The second example was a caption under a photograph of the newly engaged couple; The *Times* wanted to make sure that readers understood that 'Wall Wall' really was the young lady's surname and not a misprint!

## The Dash

Although the dash is a much maligned mark — especially by punctuation purists who decry its substitution for the colon — it has in recent times attracted a growing band of defenders. 'It's the most exciting and dramatic punctuation mark of them all!' claim some.

Primarily used to interrupt or extend a sentence, the dash is an extraordinarily versatile mark when used creatively. Here here are some of the more respectable ways in which the dash will be found useful:

- LINKING DEVICE

  Mrs Sims had four daughters — Poppy, Iris, Pansy and Petal.

- AS A PAUSE

  Everyone expected the poet to be controversial — but not to the extent of swearing at the chairwoman and falling off the stage.

- CUEING A SURPRISE

  The adhesive gave way the beard came adrift and Santa Claus was revealed as — Aunt Clara!

- NOTING AN EXCEPTION

  A straight line is the shortest distance between two points — when you're sober.

- INDICATING HESITATION

  'There will be, of course, er— a small charge, because — well, er —,

| | |
|---|---|
| • SEPARATING LISTS | She assembled all the ingredients — flour, sugar, eggs, salt, lard and raisins — and started on the pudding. |
| • AFTERTHOUGHTS | They babbled on, delighted at sighting the rare parakeet — I didn't see so much as a feather. |

Where the dash is used parenthetically — to enclose matter in much the same way as with brackets or commas — don't forget the second dash.

The sentence calls for a dash, not a comma, after luck. It's a lesson to us all — not to be slapdash with the dash!

## The Hyphen

Although both are little horizontal lines — albeit one a shade shorter than the other — hyphens and dashes are not related. A hyphen joins two or more words together.

- While a dash keeps them apart.
- What *they do have* in common is that they are inclined *to be* overused and abused.

Then there are hyphenated couples never destined to become permanent partners because of 'letter collision', which is visually disconcerting: shell-like (not shelllike); semi-illiterate (not semiilliterate); de-ice (not deice); co-wrote (not cowrote)—although we accept such unhyphenated words as cooperative and coordination.

Generally, hyphens are used after the prefixes ex:

- (ex-cop)
- non- (non-starter)
- self- (self-employed).
- anti- (antifreeze)
- counter- (counterweight)
- co- (coreligionist)
- neo- (neoclassicism)
- pre- (prehensile)
- and un- (unconditional).

But there are some exceptions: co-respondent (to distinguish it from a somewhat misspell correspondent!) and re-creation (not recreation).

## Wordbreaks and Linebreaks

Aside from helping to construct compound words, hyphens enable us to split words at the end of lines. Normally, words are split according to syllabication (or syl-lab-i-ca-tion) which follows the logic of word construction.

> *NOTE:* But it is apparent that a lot of modern typesetting follows no such rules and words are likely to be split on rather more laissez-faire principles, giving rise to such unlikely compounds as fig-urine, the-ones, should-er, condom-inium, physiotherapists, hor-semen, and mans-laughter.

## Hassle-free Hyphenating

Unfortunately the business of hyphenating is never likely to be completely hassle-free. The reason is that hyphenated and unhyphenated compound words are being created all the time and it can take a decade before there is anything like universal agreement on the final fixed form of a word.

Here is a guide to many hyphenated words and names likely to crop up in everyday usage:

- accident-prone
- acid-free
- age-old
- air-conditioning
- air-cooled
- air-dried
- all-American
- all-clear
- ankle-deep
- anti-abortion
- armour-piercing
- attorney-at-law
- awe-inspiring
- bandy-legged
- billet-doux
- bird-brain
- black-eyed
- bleary-eyed
- blood-alcohol
- blood-red
- bloody-nosed
- blue-pencil
- bone-shaking
- break-even
- break-in
- breast-fed
- brick-built
- bright-eyed
- broad-beamed
- broken-down
- brother-in-law
- bull's-eye
- burnt-out
- by-and-by
- call-up
- cane-backed
- card-index
- carpet-sweeping
- catch-as-catch-can
- cat-o'-nine-tails
- cat's-eye
- cattle-raising
- check-in
- child-proof
- city-bred
- clear-cut
- clean-shaven
- even-tempered
- ever-present
- ever-ready
- ex-husband
- ex-serviceman
- extra-large
- face-saving

- fact-finding
- fair-skinned
- far-distant
- fat-free
- father-in-law
- feeble-bodied
- fever-stricken
- fill-in
- fine-drawn
- fire-resistant
- five-ply
- flag-raising
- fiat-bottomed
- flea-bitten
- fleet-footed
- flip-flop
- fly-by-night
- follow-on
- foot-and-mouth disease
- fore-edge
- forget-me-not
- four-letter word
- four-o'clock (five-o'clock, etc)
- four-part (five-part, etc)
- free-spoken
- front-end
- full-grown
- full-strength
- fur-lined
- get-at-able
- get-together
- give-and-take
- go-ahead
- go-between
- go-getter
- God-fearing
- gold-plated
- good-for-nothing
- good-looking
- grass-roots
- ill-timed
- ill-treat
- ill-use
- in-flight
- infra-red
- Irish-born (British-born, American-born, etc)
- ivy-covered
- jack-of-all-trades
- jack-o'-lantern
- jerry-built
- jet-propelled
- jewel-studded
- jiggery-pokery
- Johnny-come-lately
- jump-start
- jury-rigged
- kiln-dry
- king-size
- kiss-and-tell
- knee-brace
- knee-deep

- knee-high
- knock-for-knock
- knock-kneed
- know-all
- know-how
- know-it-all
- lace-edged
- lady-in-waiting
- land-based
- Land-Rover
- large-scale
- late-lamented
- Latter-day Saint
- lay-by
- lean-to
- left-bank
- left-handed
- life-size
- light-footed
- light-headed
- light-year
- like-minded
- lily-white
- little-known
- little-used
- off-putting
- off-the-record
- old-fashioned
- old-maidish
- 0-level
- on-and-off
- one-night stand
- one-sided
- once-over
- open-air
- out-and-out
- out-of-date
- out-of-doors
- out-of-the-way
- over-the-counter
- pace-setting
- pale-faced
- paper-thin
- part-time
- passers-by
- penny-pinching
- pest-ridden
- photo-offset
- pick-me-up
- pigeon-toed
- pile-driving
- pitch-black
- place-name
- plain-spoken
- pleasure-bent
- pleasure-seeking
- pocket-sized
- point-to-point
- pole-vault
- post-natal
- pre-natal
- price-cutting
- price-fixing
- pro-Arab
  (pro-German, etc)
- public-spirited

- punch-drunk
- put-on
- quasi-legal
- quick-change
- quick-tempered
- quick-witted
- rat-infested
- silver-tongued
- simple-minded
- single-breasted
- single-seater
- Sino-Japanese, etc
- sister-in-law six-cylinder
- six-shooter
- skin-graft
- sky-high
- slap-up
- slow-motion
- small-scale
- snail-paced
- so-and-so
- so-called
- soft-boiled
- soft-pedal
- soft-shelled
- son-in-law
- spoon-fed
- spot-check
- spread-eagle
- stage-struck
- stand-in
- steel-framed

- stick-in-the-mud
- stick-up
- stiff-backed
- stock-still
- stone-cold
- stone-dead
- storm-tossed
- straight-backed
- straight-faced
- strong-arm
- sub-lieutenant
- sugar-coated
- sun-baked
- sun-dried
- sure-fire
- sure-footed
- swollen-headed
- T-shirt
- tail-ender
- take-home
- tax-exempt
- tax-free
- washed-out
- washed-up
- water-cooled
- water-soaked
- water-soluble
- wave-worn
- weak-kneed
- weak-willed
- weather-beaten
- weather-bound
- weather-wise

- web-footed
- week-ending
- week-old
- weigh-in
- well-being
- well-bred
- well-deserving
- well-informed
- well-known
- well-read
- well-spoken
- well-thought-of
- well-thought-out
- well-to-do
- well-wisher
- well-worn
- wet-nurse
- wide-angle
- wide-awake
- wide-open
- will-o'-the-wisp
- window-cleaning
- window-dressing
- window-shopping
- wire-haired
- wood-panelled
- word-perfect
- work-and-turn
- world-beater
- worm-eaten
- would-be
- wrong-thinking
- wych-elm

- x-ray or X-ray
- Y-chromosome
- year-old
- clear-eyed
- clip-clop
- close-knit
- closed-circuit
- Coca-Cola
- cold-shoulder
- come-on
- co-op
- copper-bottomed
- court-martial
- co-worker
- cross-channel
- cross-country
- cross-dressing
- cross-examine
- cross-purposes
- crow's-foot
- custom-tailored
- cut-throat
- daddy-longlegs
- daughter-in-law
- deaf-and-dumb
- deep-freeze
- deep-sea fishing
- dew-laden
- die-cut
- dog-eared
- do-it-yourself
- door-to-door
- double-barrel

- double-cross
- double-dealing
- double-decker
- double-entendre
- double-park
- double-quick
- double-up
- Dow-Jones
- drip-dry
- drive-in
- drug-addicted
- duck-billed
- dust-laden
- ear-splitting
- earth-shaking
- east-northeast,
- even-numbered
- grey-haired
- gun-shy
- habit-forming
- half-and-half
- half-alive
- half-baked
- half-breed
- half-hourly
- half-mast
- hard-of-hearing
- hard-on
- half-true
- half -yearly
- hand-built
- hand-in-hand
- hand-knit
- hand-me-down
- hand-out
- hand-picked
- hands-off
- hard-and-fast
- hard-hat
- hard-hit
- hard-won
- head-on
- heart-throb
- heart-to-heart
- heaven-sent
- helter-skelter
- high-class
- high-minded
- higgledy-piggledy
- high-spirited
- high-tech
- hit-and-miss
- hit-and-run
- hog-tie
- hollow-eyed
- home-baked
- horse-racing
- hot-blooded
- how-do-you-do
- ice-cold
- ice-cooled
- ice-cream cone/soda (but ice cream)
- ill-advised
- ill-fated
- long-awaited

- long-distance
- long-handled
- long-legged
- long-lived
- loose-limbed
- love-lies-bleeding
- low-key
- low-lying
- mail-order
- make-believe
- man-hours
- man-of-war
- many-coloured
- mare's-nest
- mass-produced
- May-day
- mean-spirited
- micro-organism
- middle-aged
- middle-of-the-road
- mid-Victorian (mid-forties, etc)
- mile-long
- mother-in-law
- mother-of-pearl
- motor-driven
- mouth-filling
- mud-splashed
- muu-muu
- name-dropping
- near-miss
- near-sighted
- needle-sharp
- ne'er-do-well
- never-ending
- never-never
- new-mown
- nickel-plated
- night-flying
- noble-minded
- non-starter,
- oak-beamed
- odd-job man
- odd-numbered
- off-season
- off-licence
- off-peak
- razor-keen
- razor-sharp
- re-cover (e.g. a sofa)
- ready-built
- ready-mix
- red-faced
- red-hot
- right-angle
- right-handed
- right-minded
- right-of-way
- ring-fence
- ring-in road-test
- rock-climbing
- roll-on roll-off
- Rolls-Royce
- rose-scented
- rough-and-ready
- rough-and-tumble

- rough-coat
- rubber-stamped
- run-in
- run-on
- rye-grass
- St Martin-in-the-Fields
- Saint-Saens
- sabre-toothed
- saddle-backed
- sawn-off
- say-so
- scar-faced
- second-class
- second-guess
- second-rate
- set-aside
- set-to
- sharp-witted
- shell-like
- shilly-shally
- shop-soiled
- short-changed
- short-circuited
- short-handed
- short-lived
- shut-in
- sign-on
- silver-haired
- test-tube baby
- thought-provoking
- three-cornered
- three-piece
- three-ply
- three-ring circus
- tie-break
- tight-fitting
- time-consuming
- time-honoured
- tip-off
- tom-tom
- tone-deaf
- top-hatted
- trade-in
- trans-Siberian (trans-Canadian, etc, but transatlantic — no hyphen)
- trap-door spider,
- trouble-free
- true-blue
- try-on
- twenty-first (twenty-third, forty-sixth, etc)
- tutti-frutti
- tut-tut
- twice-told
- two-faced
- two-sided
- two-step
- two-up
- U-boat
- un-American, etc
- uncalled-for
- unheard-of
- unthought-of

- up-and-coming
- U-turn
- value-added tax
- velvet-pile
- vice-chairman (but vice admiral, vice president, etc, no hyphens)
- V-neck
- voice-over
- waist-high
- walkie-talkie
- walk-in
- walk-on
- warm-hearted
- year-round
- yellow-bellied
- Y-fronts
- young-womanhood
- Z-chromosome
- zero-rated.